The Iceman Cometh

The Iceman Cometh

Eugene O'Neill

With a Foreword by
Harold Bloom

YALE NOTA BENE

Yale University Press   New Haven and London

First published as a Yale Nota Bene book in 2006.

For information about this and other Yale University Press publications, please
contact:

   U.S. office   sales.press@yale.edu
   Europe office   sales@yaleup.co.uk

Set in Garamond type by Tseng Information Systems.
Printed in the United States of America.

Library of Congress Control Number: 2006903367
ISBN-13: 978-0-300-11743-1 (pbk.)
ISBN-10: 0-300-11743-4 (pbk.)

A catalogue record for this book is available from the British Library.

10 9 8 7 6 5 4 3 2 1

Foreword

HAROLD BLOOM

I

It is an inevitable oddity that the principal American dramatist to date should have no American precursors. Eugene O'Neill's art as a playwright owes most to Strindberg's, and something crucial, though rather less, to Ibsen's. Intellectually, O'Neill's ancestry also has little to do with American tradition, with Emerson or William James or any other of our cultural speculators. Schopenhauer, Nietzsche, and Freud formed O'Neill's sense of what little was possible for any of us. Even where American literary tradition was strongest, in the novel and poetry, it did not much affect O'Neill. His novelists were Zola and Conrad; his poets were Dante Gabriel Rossetti and Swinburne. Overwhelmingly an Irish American, with his Jansenist Catholicism transformed into anger at God, he had little active interest in the greatest American writer, Whitman, though his spiritual darkness has a curious, antithetical relation to Whitman's overt analysis of our national character.

Yet O'Neill, despite his many limitations, is the most American of our handful of dramatists who matter most: Williams, Miller, Wilder, Albee, Kushner, perhaps Mamet and Shepard. A national quality that is literary, yet has no clear relation to our domestic literary traditions, is nearly always present in O'Neill's strongest works. We can recognize Hawthorne in Henry James, and Whitman (however repressed) in T. S. Eliot, while the relation of Hemingway and Faulkner to Mark Twain is just as evident as their debt to Conrad.

Besides the question of his genre (since there was no vital American drama before O'Neill), there would seem to be some hidden factor that governed O'Neill's ambiguous relation to our literary past. It was certainly not the lack of critical discernment on O'Neill's part. His admiration for Hart Crane's poetry, at its most difficult, was solely responsible for the publication of Crane's first volume, *White Buildings,* for which O'Neill initially offered to write the introduction, withdrawing in favor of Allen Tate when the impossibility of his writing a critical essay on Crane's complexities became clear to O'Neill. But to have recognized Hart Crane's genius, so early and so helpfully, testifies to O'Neill's profound insights into the American literary imagination at its strongest.

The dramatist whose masterpieces are *The Iceman Cometh* and *Long Day's Journey into Night,* and, in a class just short of those, *A Moon for the Misbegotten* and *A Touch of the Poet,* is not exactly to be regarded as a celebrator of the possibilities of American life. The central strain in our literature remains Emersonian, from Whitman to our contemporaries like Saul Bellow and John Ashbery; even the tradition that reacted against Emerson—from Poe, Hawthorne, and Melville through Gnostics of the abyss like Nathanael West and Thomas Pynchon—remains always alert to transcendental and extraordinary American possibilities. Robert Penn Warren must be the most overtly anti-Emersonian partisan in our history, yet even Warren seeks an American Sublime in his still-ongoing poetry. O'Neill would appear to be the most non-Emersonian author of any eminence in our literature. Irish-American through and through, with an heroic resentment of the New England Yankee tradition, O'Neill from the start seemed to know that his spiritual quest was to undermine Emerson's American religion of self-reliance.

O'Neill's own Irish Jansenism is curiously akin to the New England Puritanism he opposed, but that only increased the rancor of his powerful polemic in *Desire under the Elms, Mourning Becomes Electra,* and *More Stately Mansions.* The Will to Live is set against New England Puritanism in what O'Neill himself once called "the battle of moral forces in the New England scene" to which he said he felt closest as an artist. But since this is Schopenhauer's rapacious Will to Live, and not Bernard Shaw's genial revision of that

Will into the Life Force of a benign Creative Evolution, O'Neill is in the terrible position of opposing one death-drive with another. Only the inescapable Strindberg comes to mind as a visionary quite as negative as O'Neill, so that *The Iceman Cometh* might as well have been called *The Dance of Death,* and *Long Day's Journey into Night* could be retitled *The Ghost Sonata.* O'Neill's most powerful self-representations—as Edmund in *Long Day's Journey* and Larry Slade in *Iceman*—are astonishingly negative identifications, particularly in an American context.

Edmund and Slade do not long for death in the mode of Whitman and his descendants—Wallace Stevens, T. S. Eliot, Hart Crane, and Theodore Roethke—all of whom tend to incorporate the image of a desired death into the great, triple trope of night, the mother, and the sea. Edmund Tyrone and Larry Slade long to die because life without transcendence is impossible, and yet transcendence is totally unavailable. O'Neill's true polemic against his country and its spiritual tradition is not, as he insisted, that "its main idea is that everlasting game of trying to possess your own soul by the possession of something outside it." Though uttered in 1946, in remarks before the first performance of *The Iceman Cometh,* such a reflection is banal and represents a weak misreading of *The Iceman Cometh.* The play's true argument is that your own soul cannot be possessed, whether by possessing something or someone outside it, or by joining yourself to a transcendental possibility, to whatever version of an Emersonian Oversoul that you might prefer. The United States, in O'Neill's dark view, was uniquely the country that had refused to learn the truths of the spirit, which is that good and the means of good, love and the means of love, are irreconcilable.

Such a formulation is Shelleyan, and reminds one of O'Neill's High Romantic inheritance, which reached him through pre-Raphaelite poetry and literary speculation. O'Neill seems a strange instance of the Aestheticism of Rossetti and Pater, but his metaphysical nihilism, desperate faith in art, and phantasmagoric naturalism stem directly from them. When Jamie Tyrone quotes from Rossetti's "Willowwood" sonnets, he gives the epigraph not only to *Long Day's Journey* but to all of O'Neill: "Look into my face. My name is Might-Have-Been; / I am also called No More, Too Late,

Farewell." In O'Neill's deepest polemic, the lines are quoted by, and for, all Americans of imagination whatsoever.

I I

Like its great precursor play, Strindberg's *The Dance of Death*, O'Neill's *The Iceman Cometh* must be one of the most remorseless of what purport to be tragic dramas since the Greeks and the Jacobeans. Whatever tragedy meant to the incredibly harsh Strindberg, to O'Neill it had to possess a "transfiguring nobility," presumably that of the artist like O'Neill himself in his relation to his time and his country, of which he observed that: "we are tragedy, the most appalling yet written or unwritten." O'Neill's strength was never conceptual, and so we are not likely to render his stances into a single coherent view of tragedy.

Whiteman could say that "these States are themselves the greatest poem," and we know what he meant, but I do not know how to read O'Neill's "we are tragedy." When I suffer through the *New York Times* every morning, am I reading tragedy? Does *The Iceman Cometh* manifest a "transfiguring nobility?" How could it? Are Larry Slade in *Iceman* or Edmund Tyrone in *Long Day's Journey into Night*, both clearly O'Neill's surrogates, either of them tragic in relation to their time and country? Or to ask all this in a single question: are the crippling sorrows of what Freud called "family romances" tragic or are they not primarily instances of strong pathos, reductive process that cannot, by definition, manifest an authentic "transfiguring nobility?"

I think that we need to ignore O'Neill on tragedy if we are to learn to watch and read *The Iceman Cometh* for the dramatic values it certainly possesses. Its principal limitation, I suspect, stems from its tendentious assumption that "we are tragedy," that "these States" have become the "most appalling" of tragedies. Had O'Neill survived into our present age and observed our Yuppies on the march, doubtless he would have been even more appalled. But societies are not dramas, and O'Neill was not Jeremiah the prophet. His strength was neither in stance nor style, but in the dramatic representation of illusions and despairs, in the persuasive imitation of human personality, particularly in its self-destructive weaknesses.

Critics have rightly emphasized how important O'Neill's lapsed Irish Catholicism was to him and to his plays. But "importance" is a perplexing notion in this context. Certainly the absence of the Roman Catholic faith is the given condition of *The Iceman Cometh.* Yet we would do O'Neill's play wrong if we retitled it *Waiting for the Iceman,* and tried to assimilate it to the Gnostic cosmos of Samuel Beckett, just as we would destroy *Long Day's Journey into Night* if we retitled it *Endgame in New London.* All that O'Neill and Beckett have in common is Schopenhauer, with whom they share a Gnostic sense that our world is a great emptiness, the *kenoma,* as the Gnostics of the second century of the Common Era called it. But Beckett's post-Protestant cosmos could not be redeemed by the descent of the alien god. O'Neill's post-Catholic world longs for the suffering Christ, and is angry at him for not returning. Such a longing is by no means in itself dramatic, unlike Beckett's ironically emptied-out cosmos.

A comparison of O'Neill to Beckett is hardly fair, since Beckett is infinitely the better artist, subtler mind, and finer stylist. Beckett writes apocalyptic farce, or tragicomedy raised to its greatest eminence. O'Neill doggedly tells his one story and one story only, and his story turns out to be himself. *The Iceman Cometh,* being O'Neill at his most characteristic, raises the vexed question of whether and just how dramatic value can survive a paucity of eloquence, too much commonplace religiosity, and a thorough lack of understanding of the perverse complexities of human nature. Plainly *Iceman* does survive, and so does *Long Day's Journey.* They stage remarkably, and hold me in the audience, though they give neither aesthetic pleasure nor spiritually memorable pain when I reread them in the study.

For sheer bad writing, O'Neill's only rival among significant American authors is Theodore Dreiser, whose *Sister Carrie* and *An American Tragedy* demonstrate a similar ability to evade the consequences of rhetorical failure. Dreiser has some dramatic effectiveness, but his peculiar strength appears to be mythic. O'Neill, unquestionably a dramatist of genius, fails also on the mythic level; his anger against God, or the absence of God, remains petulant and personal, and his attempt to universalize that anger by turning it against his country's failure to achieve spiritual reality is simply misguided.

No country, by definition, achieves anything spiritual anyway. We live and die, in the spirit, in solitude, and the true strength of *Iceman* is its intense dramatic exemplification of that somber reality.

Whether the confessional impulse in O'Neill's later plays ensued from Catholic *praxis* is beyond my surmise, though John Henry Raleigh and other critics have urged this view. I suspect that here too the influence of the non-Catholic Strindberg was decisive. A harsh expressionism dominates *Iceman* and *Long Day's Journey,* where the terrible confessions are not made to priestly surrogates but to fellow sinners, and with no hopes of absolution. Confession becomes another station on the way to death, whether by suicide, or by alcohol, or by other modes of slow decay.

Iceman's strength is in three of its figures: Hickman (Hickey), Slade, and Parritt, of whom only Slade is due to survive, though in a minimal sense. Hickey, who preaches nihilism, is a desperate self-deceiver and so a deceiver of others, in his self-appointed role as evangelist of the abyss. Slade, evasive and solipsistic, works his way to a more authentic nihilism than Hickey's. Poor Parritt, young and self-haunted, cannot achieve the sense of nothingness that would save him from Puritanical self-condemnation.

Life, in *Iceman,* is what it is in Schopenhauer: illusion. Hickey, once a great sustainer of illusions, arrives in the company of "the Iceman of Death," hardly the "sane and sacred death" of Whitman, but insane and impious death, our death. One feels the refracted influence of Ibsen in Hickey's twisted deidealizings, but Hickey is an Ibsen protagonist in the last ditch. He does not destroy others in his quest to destroy illusions, but only himself. His judgments of Harry Hope's patrons are intended not to liberate them but to teach his old friends to accept and live with failure. Yet Hickey, though pragmatically wrong, means only to have done good. In an understanding strangely akin to Wordsworth's in the sublime *Tale of Margaret* (*The Ruined Cottage*), Hickey sees that we are destroyed by vain hope more inexorably than by the anguish of total despair. And that is where I would locate the authentic mode of tragedy in *Iceman.* It is Hickey's tragedy, rather than Slade's (O'Neill's), because Hickey is slain between right and right, as in the Hegelian theory of tragedy.

To deprive the derelicts of hope is right, and to sustain them in their illusory "pipe dreams" is right also.

Caught between right and right, Hickey passes into phantasmagoria, and in that compulsive condition he makes the ghastly confession that he murdered his unhappy, dreadfully saintly wife. His motive, he asserts perversely, was love, but here too he is caught between antitheses, and we are not able to interpret with certainty whether he was more moved by love or hatred:

HICKEY
Simply.
So I killed her.
There is a moment of dead silence. Even the detectives are caught in it and stand motionless.

PARRITT
Suddenly gives up and relaxes limply in his chair—in a low voice in which there is a strange exhausted relief.
I may as well confess, Larry. There's no use lying any more. You know, anyway. I didn't give a damn about the money. It was because I hated her.

HICKEY
Obliviously.
And then I saw I'd always known that was the only possible way to give her peace and free her from the misery of loving me. I saw it meant peace for me, too, knowing she was at peace. I felt as though a ton of guilt was lifted off my mind. I remember I stood by the bed and suddenly I had to laugh. I couldn't help it, and I knew Evelyn would forgive me. I remember I heard myself speaking to her, as if it was something I'd always wanted to say: "Well, you know what you can do with your pipe dream now, you damned bitch!"
He stops with a horrified start, as if shocked out of a nightmare, as if he couldn't believe he heard what he had just said. He stammers.
No! I never—!

PARRITT
To LARRY—*sneeringly.*

Yes, that's it! Her and the damned old Movement pipe dream! Eh, Larry?

HICKEY
Bursts into frantic denial.
No! That's a lie! I never said—! Good God, I couldn't have said that! If I did, I'd gone insane! Why, I loved Evelyn better than anything in life!
He appeals brokenly to the crowd.
Boys, you're all my old pals! You've known old Hickey for years! You know I'd never—
His eyes fix on HOPE.
You've known me longer than anyone, Harry. You know I must have been insane, don't you, Governor?

Rather than a demystifier, whether of self or others, Hickey is revealed as a tragic enigma, who cannot sell himself a coherent account of the horror he has accomplished. Did he slay Evelyn because of a hope—hers or his—or because of a mutual despair? He does not know, nor does O'Neill, nor do we. Nor does anyone know why Parritt betrayed his mother, the anarchist activist, and her comrades and his. Slade condemns Parritt to a suicide's death, but without persuading us that he has uncovered the motive for so hideous a betrayal. Caught in a moral dialectic of guilt and suffering, Parritt appears to be entirely a figure of pathos, without the weird idealism that makes Hickey an interesting instance of High Romantic tragedy.

Parritt at least provokes analysis; the drama's failure is Larry Slade, much against O'Neill's palpable intentions, which were to move his surrogate from contemplation to action. Slade ought to end poised on the threshold of a religious meditation on the vanity of life in a world from which God is absent. But his final speech, expressing a reaction to Parritt's suicide, is the weakest in the play:

LARRY
In a whisper of horrified pity.
Poor devil!
A long-forgotten faith returns to him for a moment and he mumbles.

God rest his soul in peace.

He opens his eyes—with a bitter self-derision.

Ah, the damned pity—the wrong kind, as Hickey said! Be God, there's no hope! I'll never be a success in the grandstand—or anywhere else! Life is too much for me! I'll be a weak fool looking with pity at the two sides of everything till the day I die!

With an intense bitter sincerity.

May that day come soon!

He pauses startledly, surprised at himself—then with a sardonic grin.

Be God, I'm the only real convert to death Hickey made here. From the bottom of my coward's heart I mean that now!

The momentary return of Catholicism is at variance with the despair of the death-drive here, and Slade does not understand that he has not been converted to any sense of death, at all. His only strength would be in emulating Hickey's tragic awareness between right and right, but of course without following Hickey into violence: "I'll be a weak fool looking with pity at the two sides of everything till the day I die!" That vision of the two sides, with compassion, is the only hope worthy of the dignity of any kind of tragic conception. O'Neill ended by exemplifying Yeats's great apothegm: he could embody the truth, but he could not know it.

The Iceman Cometh

Characters

HARRY HOPE, *proprietor of a saloon and rooming house**

ED MOSHER, *Hope's brother-in-law, one-time circus man**

PAT MCGLOIN, *one-time Police Lieutenant**

WILLIE OBAN, *a Harvard Law School alumnus**

JOE MOTT, *one-time proprietor of a Negro gambling house*

PIET WETJOEN ("THE GENERAL"),
*one-time leader of a Boer commando**

CECIL LEWIS ("THE CAPTAIN"),
*one-time Captain of British infantry**

JAMES CAMERON ("JIMMY TOMORROW"),
*one-time Boer War correspondent**

HUGO KALMAR, *one-time editor of Anarchist periodicals*

LARRY SLADE, *one-time Syndicalist-Anarchist**

ROCKY PIOGGI, *night bartender**

*Roomers at Harry Hope's.

DON PARRITT*

PEARL*

MARGIE*   } street walkers

CORA

CHUCK MORELLO, *day bartender**

THEODORE HICKMAN (HICKEY), *a hardware salesman*

MORAN

LIEB

Scenes

Harry Hope's is a Raines-Law hotel of the period, a cheap ginmill of the five-cent whiskey, last-resort variety situated on the downtown West Side of New York. The building, owned by Hope, is a narrow five-story structure of the tenement type, the second floor a flat occupied by the proprietor. The renting of rooms on the upper floors, under the Raines-Law loopholes, makes the establishment legally a hotel and gives it the privilege of serving liquor in the back room of the bar after closing hours and on Sundays, provided a meal is served with the booze, thus making a back room legally a hotel restaurant. This food provision was generally circumvented by putting a property sandwich in the middle of each table, an old desiccated ruin of dust-laden bread and mummified ham or cheese which only the drunkest yokel from the sticks ever regarded as anything but a noisome table decoration. But at Harry Hope's, Hope being a former minor Tammanyite and still possessing friends, this food technicality is ignored as irrelevant, except during the fleeting alarms of reform agitation. Even Hope's back room is not a separate room, but simply the rear of the barroom divided from the bar by drawing a dirty black curtain across the room.

Act One

SCENE

The back room and a section of the bar of HARRY HOPE'S *saloon on an early morning in summer, 1912. The right wall of the back room is a dirty black curtain which separates it from the bar. At rear, this curtain is drawn back from the wall so the bartender can get in and out. The back room is crammed with round tables and chairs placed so close together that it is a difficult squeeze to pass between them. In the middle of the rear wall is a door opening on a hallway. In the left corner, built out into the room, is the toilet with a sign "This is it" on the door. Against the middle of the left wall is a nickel-in-the-slot phonograph. Two windows, so glazed with grime one cannot see through them, are in the left wall, looking out on a backyard. The walls and ceiling once were white, but it was a long time ago, and they are now so splotched, peeled, stained and dusty that their color can best be described as dirty. The floor, with iron spittoons placed here and there, is covered with sawdust. Lighting comes from single wall brackets, two at left and two at rear.*

There are three rows of tables, from front to back. Three are in the front line. The one at left-front has four chairs; the one at center-front, four; the one at right-front, five. At rear of, and half between, front tables one and two is a table of the second row with five chairs. A table, similarly placed at rear of front tables two and three, also has five chairs. The third row of tables, four chairs to one and six to the other, is against the rear wall on either side of the door.

At right of this dividing curtain is a section of the barroom, with the end of the bar seen at rear, a door to the hall at left of it. At front is a table with four chairs. Light comes from the street windows off right, the gray subdued light of early morning in a narrow street. In the back room, LARRY SLADE *and* HUGO KALMAR *are at the table at left-front,* HUGO *in a chair facing right,* LARRY *at rear of table facing front, with an empty chair between them. A fourth chair is at right of table, facing left.* HUGO *is a small an in his late fifties. He has a head much too big for his body, a high forehead, crinkly long black hair streaked with gray, a square face with a pug nose, a walrus mustache, black eyes which peer near-sightedly from behind thick-lensed spectacles, tiny hands and feet. He is dressed in threadbare black clothes and his white shirt is frayed at collar and cuffs, but everything about him is fastidiously clean. Even his flowing Windsor tie is neatly tied. There is a foreign atmosphere about him, the stamp of an alien radical, a strong resemblance to the type Anarchist as portrayed, bomb in hand, in newspaper cartoons. He is asleep now, bent forward in his chair, his arms folded on the table, his head resting sideways on his arms.*

LARRY SLADE *is sixty. He is tall, raw-boned, with coarse straight white hair, worn long and raggedly cut. He has a gaunt Irish face with a big nose, high cheekbones, a lantern jaw with a week's stubble of beard, a mystic's meditative pale-blue eyes with a gleam of sharp sardonic humor in them. As slovenly as* HUGO *is neat, his clothes are dirty and much slept in. His gray flannel shirt, open at the neck, has the appearance of having never been washed. From the way he methodically scratches himself with his long-fingered, hairy hands, he is lousy and reconciled to being so. He is the only occupant of the room who is not asleep. He stares in front of him, an expression of tired tolerance giving his face the quality of a pitying but weary old priest's.*

All four chairs at the middle table, front, are occupied. JOE MOTT *sits at left-front of the table, facing front. Behind him, facing right-front, is* PIET WETJOEN *("The General"). At center of the table, rear,* JAMES CAMERON *("Jimmy Tomorrow") sits facing front. At right of table, opposite* JOE, *is* CECIL LEWIS *("The Captain").*

JOE MOTT *is a Negro, about fifty years old, brown-skinned, stocky, wearing a light suit that had once been flashily sporty but is now about to fall apart. His pointed tan buttoned shoes, faded pink shirt and bright tie belong to the same vintage. Still, he manages to preserve an atmosphere of nattiness and there is nothing dirty about his appearance. His face is only mildly negroid in type. The nose is thin and his lips are not noticeably thick. His hair is crinkly and he is beginning to get bald. A scar from a knife slash runs from his left cheekbone to jaw. His face would be hard and tough if it were not for its good nature and lazy humor. He is asleep, his nodding head supported by his left hand.*

PIET WETJOEN, *the Boer, is in his fifties, a huge man with a bald head and a long grizzled beard. He is slovenly dressed in a dirty shapeless patched suit, spotted by food. A Dutch farmer type, his once great muscular strength has been debauched into flaccid tallow. But despite his blubbery mouth and sodden bloodshot blue eyes, there is still a suggestion of old authority lurking in him like a memory of the drowned. He is hunched forward, both elbows on the table, his hand on each side of his head for support.*

JAMES CAMERON *("Jimmy Tomorrow") is about the same size and age as* HUGO, *a small man. Like* HUGO, *he wears threadbare black, and everything about him is clean. But the resemblance ceases there.* JIMMY *has a face like an old well-bred, gentle bloodhound's, with folds of flesh hanging from each side of his mouth, and big brown friendly guileless eyes, more bloodshot than any bloodhound's ever were. He has mouse-colored thinning hair, a little bulbous nose, buck teeth in a small rabbit mouth. But his forehead is fine, his eyes are intelligent and there once was a competent ability in him. His speech is educated, with the ghost of a Scotch rhythm in it. His manners are those of a gentleman. There is a quality about him of a prim, Victorian old maid, and at the same time of a likable, affectionate boy who has never grown up. He sleeps, chin on chest, hands folded in his lap.*

CECIL LEWIS *("The Captain") is as obviously English as Yorkshire pudding and just as obviously the former army officer. He is going on sixty. His hair and military mustache are white, his eyes bright blue, his complexion that of a turkey. His lean figure is still erect and square-shouldered. He is stripped to the waist, his coat, shirt, undershirt, collar and tie crushed up into a pillow on the table in front of him, his head side-ways on this pillow, facing front, his arms dangling toward the floor. On his lower left shoulder is the big ragged scar of an old wound.*

At the table at right, front, HARRY HOPE, *the proprietor, sits in the middle, facing front, with* PAT MCGLOIN *on his right and* ED MOSHER *on his left, the other two chairs being unoccupied.*

Both MCGLOIN *and* MOSHER *are big paunchy men.* MCGLOIN *has his old occupation of policeman stamped all over him. He is in his fifties, sandy-haired, bullet-headed, jowly, with protruding ears and little round eyes. His face must once have been brutal and greedy, but time and whiskey have melted it down into a good-humored, parasite's character-lessness. He wears old clothes and is slovenly. He is slumped sideways on his chair, his head drooping jerkily toward one shoulder.*

ED MOSHER *is going on sixty. He has a round kewpie's face—a kew-pie who is an unshaven habitual drunkard. He looks like an enlarged, elderly, bald edition of the village fat boy—a sly fat boy, congenitally indolent, a practical joker, a born grafter and con merchant. But amus-ing and essentially harmless, even in his most enterprising days, because always too lazy to carry crookedness beyond petty swindling. The influ-ence of his old circus career is apparent in his get-up. His worn clothes are flashy; he wears phony rings and a heavy brass watch-chain (not con-nected to a watch). Like* MCGLOIN, *he is slovenly. His head is thrown back, his big mouth open.*

HARRY HOPE *is sixty, white-haired, so thin the description "bag of bones" was made for him. He has the face of an old family horse, prone to tantrums, with balkiness always smoldering in its wall eyes, waiting for any excuse to shy and pretend to take the bit in its teeth. Hope is one of those men whom everyone likes on sight, a softhearted slob, without malice, feeling superior to no one, a sinner among sinners, a born easy mark for every appeal. He attempts to hide his defenselessness behind a testy truculent manner, but this has never fooled anyone. He is a little deaf, but not half as deaf as he sometimes pretends. His sight is failing but is not as bad as he complains it is. He wears five-and-ten-cent-store spectacles which are so out of alignment that one eye at times peers half over one glass while the other eye looks half under the other. He has badly fitting store teeth, which click like castanets when he begins to fume. He is dressed in an old coat from one suit and pants from another.*

In a chair facing right at the table in the second line, between the first two tables, front, sits WILLIE OBAN, *his head on his left arm outstretched along the table edge. He is in his late thirties, of average height, thin. His haggard, dissipated face has a small nose, a pointed chin, blue eyes with colorless lashes and brows. His blond hair, badly in need of a cut, clings in a limp part to his skull. His eyelids flutter continually as if any light were too strong for his eyes. The clothes he wears belong on a scarecrow. They seem constructed of an inferior grade of dirty blotting paper. His shoes are even more disreputable, wrecks of imitation leather, one laced with twine, the other with a bit of wire. He has no socks, and his bare feet show through holes in the soles, with his big toes sticking out of the uppers. He keeps muttering and twitching in his sleep.*

As the curtain rises, ROCKY, *the night bartender, comes from the bar through the curtain and stands looking over the back room. He is a Neapolitan-American in his late twenties, squat and muscular, with a flat, swarthy face and beady eyes. The sleeves of his collarless shirt are rolled up on his thick, powerful arms and he wears a soiled apron. A tough guy but sentimental, in his way, and good-natured. He signals to* LARRY *with a cautious "Sstt" and motions him to see if* HOPE *is asleep.* LARRY *rises from his chair to look at* HOPE *and nods to* ROCKY. ROCKY *goes back in the bar but immediately returns with a bottle of bar whiskey and a glass. He squeezes between the tables to* LARRY.

ROCKY
In a low voice out of the side of his mouth.
Make it fast.
LARRY *pours a drink and gulps it down.* ROCKY *takes the bottle and puts it on the table where* WILLIE OBAN *is.*
Don't want de Boss to get wise when he's got one of his tightwad buns on.
He chuckles with an amused glance at HOPE.

Jees, ain't de old bastard a riot when he starts dat bull about turnin' over a new leaf? "Not a damned drink on de house," he tells me, "and all dese bums got to pay up deir room rent. Beginnin' tomorrow," he says. Jees, yuh'd tink he meant it!

He sits down in the chair at LARRY's *left.*

LARRY
Grinning.
I'll be glad to pay up—tomorrow. And I know my fellow inmates will promise the same. They've all a touching credulity concerning tomorrows.
A half-drunken mockery in his eyes.
It'll be a great day for them, tomorrow—the Feast of All Fools, with brass bands playing! Their ships will come in, loaded to the gunwales with cancelled regrets and promises fulfilled and clean slates and new leases!

ROCKY
Cynically.
Yeah, and a ton of hop!

LARRY
Leans toward him, a comical intensity in his low voice.
Don't mock the faith! Have you no respect for religion, you unregenerate Wop? What's it matter if the truth is that their favoring breeze has the stink of nickel whiskey on its breath, and their sea is a growler of lager and ale, and their ships are long since looted and scuttled and sunk on the bottom? To hell with the truth! As the history of the world proves, the truth has no bearing on anything. It's irrelevant and immaterial, as the lawyers say. The lie of a pipe dream is what gives life to the whole misbegotten mad lot of us, drunk or sober. And that's enough philosophic wisdom to give you for one drink of rot-gut.

ROCKY
Grins kiddingly.
De old Foolosopher, like Hickey calls yuh, ain't yuh? I s'pose you don't fall for no pipe dream?

LARRY

A bit stiffly.

I don't, no. Mine are all dead and buried behind me. What's before me is the comforting fact that death is a fine long sleep, and I'm damned tired, and it can't come too soon for me.

ROCKY

Yeah, just hangin' around hopin' you'll croak, ain't yuh? Well, I'm bettin' you'll have a good long wait. Jees, somebody'll have to take an axe to croak you!

LARRY

Grins.

Yes, it's my bad luck to be cursed with an iron constitution that even Harry's booze can't corrode.

ROCKY

De old anarchist wise guy dat knows all de answers! Dat's you, huh?

LARRY

Frowns.

Forget the anarchist part of it. I'm through with the Movement long since. I saw men didn't want to be saved from themselves, for that would mean they'd have to give up greed, and they'll never pay that price for liberty. So I said to the world, God bless all here, and may the best man win and die of gluttony! And I took a seat in the grand-stand of philosophical detachment to fall asleep observing the can-nibals do their death dance.

He chuckles at his own fancy—reaches over and shakes Hugo's shoulder.

Ain't I telling him the truth, Comrade Hugo?

ROCKY

Aw, fer Chris' sake, don't get dat bughouse bum started!

HUGO

Raises his head and peers at ROCKY *blearily through his thick spec-tacles—in a guttural declamatory tone.*

Capitalist swine! Bourgeois stool pigeons! Have the slaves no right to sleep even?

Then he grins at ROCKY *and his manner changes to a giggling, whee-dling playfulness, as though he were talking to a child.*

Hello, leedle Rocky! Leedle monkey-face! Vere is your leedle slave girls?

With an abrupt change to a bullying tone.

Don't be a fool! Loan me a dollar! Damned bourgeois Wop! The great Malatesta is my good friend! Buy me a trink!

He seems to run down, and is overcome by drowsiness. His head sinks to the table again and he is at once fast asleep.

ROCKY

He's out again.

More exasperated than angry.

He's lucky no one don't take his cracks serious or he'd wake up every mornin' in a hospital.

LARRY

Regarding HUGO *with pity.*

No. No one takes him seriously. That's his epitaph. Not even the comrades any more. If I've been through with the Movement long since, it's been through with him, and, thanks to whiskey, he's the only one doesn't know it.

ROCKY

I've let him get by wid too much. He's goin' to pull dat slave-girl stuff on me once too often.

His manner changes to defensive argument.

Hell, yuh'd tink I wuz a pimp or somethin'. Everybody knows me knows I ain't. A pimp don't hold no job. I'm a bartender. Dem tarts, Margie and Poil, dey're just a side line to pick up some extra dough. Strictly business, like dey was fighters and I was deir manager, see? I fix the cops fer dem so's dey can hustle widout gettin' pinched. Hell, dey'd be on de Island most of de time if it wasn't fer me. And I don't beat dem up like a pimp would. I treat dem fine. Dey like me. We're pals, see? What if I do take deir dough? Dey'd on'y trow it away. Tarts can't hang on to dough. But I'm a bartender and I work hard for my livin' in dis dump. You know dat, Larry.

LARRY

With inner sardonic amusement—flatteringly.

A shrewd business man, who doesn't miss any opportunity to get on in the world. That's what I'd call you.

ROCKY

Pleased.

Sure ting. Dat's me. Grab another ball, Larry.

LARRY *pours a drink from the bottle on* WILLIE'S *table and gulps it down.* ROCKY *glances around the room.*

Yuh'd never tink all dese bums had a good bed upstairs to go to. Scared if dey hit the hay dey wouldn't be here when Hickey showed up, and dey'd miss a coupla drinks. Dat's what kept you up too, ain't it?

LARRY

It is. But not so much the hope of booze, if you can believe that. I've got the blues and Hickey's a great one to make a joke of everything and cheer you up.

ROCKY

Yeah, some kidder! Remember how he woiks up dat gag about his wife, when he's cockeyed, cryin' over her picture and den springin' it on yuh all of a sudden dat he left her in de hay wid de iceman? *He laughs.*

I wonder what's happened to him. Yuh could set your watch by his periodicals before dis. Always got here a coupla days before Harry's birthday party, and now he's on'y got till tonight to make it. I hope he shows soon. Dis dump is like de morgue wid all dese bums passed out.

WILLIE OBAN *jerks and twitches in his sleep and begins to mumble. They watch him.*

WILLIE

Blurts from his dream.

It's a lie!

Miserably.

Papa! Papa!

LARRY

Poor devil.

Then angry with himself.

But to hell with pity! It does no good. I'm through with it!

ROCKY

Dreamin' about his old man. From what de old-timers say, de old gent sure made a pile of dough in de bucket-shop game before de cops got him.

He considers WILLIE *frowningly.*

Jees, I've seen him bad before but never dis bad. Look at dat get-up. Been playin' de old reliever game. Sold his suit and shoes at Solly's two days ago. Solly give him two bucks and a bum outfit. Yesterday he sells de bum one back to Solly for four bits and gets dese rags to put on. Now he's through. Dat's Solly's final edition he wouldn't take back for nuttin'. Willie sure is on de bottom. I ain't never seen no one so bad, except Hickey on de end of a coupla his bats.

LARRY

Sardonically.

It's a great game, the pursuit of happiness.

ROCKY

Harry don't know what to do about him. He called up his old lady's lawyer like he always does when Willie gets licked. Yuh remember dey used to send down a private dick to give him the rush to a cure, but de lawyer tells Harry nix, de old lady's off of Willie for keeps dis time and he can go to hell.

LARRY

Watches WILLIE, *who is shaking in his sleep like an old dog.*

There's the consolation that he hasn't far to go!

As if replying to this, WILLIE *comes to a crisis of jerks and moans.*

LARRY *adds in a comically intense, crazy whisper.*

Be God, he's knocking on the door right now!

WILLIE

Suddenly yells in his nightmare.

It's a God-damned lie!

He begins to sob.
Oh, Papa! Jesus!
All the occupants of the room stir on their chairs but none of them wakes up except HOPE.

ROCKY
Grabs his shoulder and shakes him.
Hey, you! Nix! Cut out de noise!
WILLIE *opens his eyes to stare around him with a bewildered horror.*

HOPE
Opens one eye to peer over his spectacles — drowsily.
Who's that yelling?

ROCKY
Willie, Boss. De Brooklyn boys is after him.

HOPE
Querulously.
Well, why don't you give the poor feller a drink and keep him quiet?
Bejees, can't I get a wink of sleep in my own back room?

ROCKY
Indignantly to LARRY.
Listen to that blind-eyed, deef old bastard, will yuh? He give me strict orders not to let Willie hang up no more drinks, no matter—

HOPE
Mechanically puts a hand to his ear in the gesture of deafness.
What's that? I can't hear you.
Then drowsily irascible.
You're a cockeyed liar. Never refused a drink to anyone needed it bad in my life! Told you to use your judgment. Ought to know better. You're too busy thinking up ways to cheat me. Oh, I ain't as blind as you think. I can still see a cash register, bejees!

ROCKY
Grins at him affectionately now — flatteringly.
Sure, Boss. Swell chance of foolin' you!

HOPE

I'm wise to you and your sidekick, Chuck. Bejees, you're burglars, not barkeeps! Blind-eyed, deef old bastard, am I? Oh, I heard you! Heard you often when you didn't think. You and Chuck laughing behind my back, telling people you throw the money up in the air and whatever sticks to the ceiling is my share! A fine couple of crooks! You'd steal the pennies off your dead mother's eyes!

ROCKY

Winks at LARRY.

Aw, Harry, me and Chuck was on'y kiddin'.

HOPE

More drowsily.

I'll fire both of you, Bejees, if you think you can play me for an easy mark, you've come to the wrong house. No one ever played Harry Hope for a sucker!

ROCKY

To LARRY.

No one but everybody.

HOPE

His eyes shut again—mutters.

Least you could do—keep things quiet—

He falls asleep.

WILLIE

Pleadingly.

Give me a drink, Rocky. Harry said it was all right. God, I need a drink.

ROCKY

Den grab it. It's right under your nose.

WILLIE

Avidly.

Thanks.

He takes the bottle with both twitching hands and tilts it to his lips and gulps down the whiskey in big swallows.

ROCKY

Sharply.

When! When!

He grabs the bottle.

I didn't say, take a bath!

Showing the bottle to LARRY—*indignantly.*

Jees, look! He's killed a half pint or more!

He turns on WILLIE *angrily, but* WILLIE *has closed his eyes and is sitting quietly, shuddering, waiting for the effect.*

LARRY

With a pitying glance.

Leave him be, the poor devil. A half pint of that dynamite in one swig will fix him for a while—if it doesn't kill him.

ROCKY

Shrugs his shoulders and sits down again.

Aw right by me. It ain't my booze.

Behind him, in the chair at left of the middle table, JOE MOTT, *the Negro, has been waking up.*

JOE

His eyes blinking sleepily.

Whose booze? Gimme some. I don't care whose. Where's Hickey? Ain't he come yet? What time's it, Rocky?

ROCKY

Gettin' near time to open up. Time you begun to sweep up in de bar.

JOE

Lazily.

Never mind de time. If Hickey ain't come, it's time Joe goes to sleep again. I was dreamin' Hickey come in de door, crackin' one of dem drummer's jokes, wavin' a big bankroll and we was all goin' be drunk for two weeks. Wake up and no luck.

Suddenly his eyes open wide.

Wait a minute, dough. I got idea. Say, Larry, how 'bout dat young guy, Parritt, came to look you up last night and rented a room? Where's he at?

LARRY

Up in his room, asleep. No hope in him, anyway, Joe. He's broke.

JOE

Dat what he told you? Me and Rocky knows different. Had a roll when he paid you his room rent, didn't he, Rocky? I seen it.

ROCKY

Yeah. He flashed it like he forgot and den tried to hide it quick.

LARRY

Surprised and resentful.

He did, did he?

ROCKY

Yeah, I figgered he don't belong, but he said he was a friend of yours.

LARRY

He's a liar. I wouldn't know him if he hadn't told me who he was. His mother and I were friends years ago on the Coast.

He hesitates—then lowering his voice.

You've read in the papers about that bombing on the Coast when several people got killed? Well, the one woman they pinched, Rosa Parritt, is his mother. They'll be coming up for trial soon, and there's no chance for them. She'll get life, I think. I'm telling you this so you'll know why if Don acts a bit queer, and not jump on him. He must be hard hit. He's her only kid.

ROCKY

Nods—then thoughtfully.

Why ain't he out dere stickin' by her?

LARRY

Frowns.

Don't ask questions. Maybe there's a good reason.

ROCKY

Stares at him—understandingly.

Sure. I get it.

Then wonderingly.

But den what kind of a sap is he to hang on to his right name?

LARRY

Irritably.

I'm telling you I don't know anything and I don't want to know. To hell with the Movement and all connected with it! I'm out of it, and everything else, and damned glad to be.

ROCKY

Shrugs his shoulders—indifferently.

Well, don't tink I'm interested in dis Parritt guy. He's nuttin' to me.

JOE

Me neider. If dere's one ting more'n anudder I cares nuttin' about, it's de sucker game you and Hugo call de Movement.

He chuckles—reminiscently.

Reminds me of damn fool argument me and Mose Porter has de udder night. He's drunk and I'm drunker. He says, "Socialist and Anarchist, we ought to shoot dem dead. Dey's all no-good sons of bitches." I says, "Hold on, you talk 's if Anarchists and Socialists was de same." "Dey is," he says. "Dey's both no-good bastards." "No, dey ain't," I says. "I'll explain the difference. De Anarchist he never works. He drinks but he never buys, and if he do ever get a nickel, he blows it in on bombs, and he wouldn't give you nothin'. So go ahead and shoot him. But de Socialist, sometimes, he's got a job, and if he gets ten bucks, he's bound by his religion to split fifty-fifty wid you. You say—how about my cut, Comrade? And you gets de five. So you don't shoot no Socialists while I'm around. Dat is, not if dey got anything. Of course, if dey's broke, den dey's no-good bastards, too."

He laughs, immensely tickled.

LARRY

Grins with sardonic appreciation.

Be God, Joe, you've got all the beauty of human nature and the practical wisdom of the world in that little parable.

ROCKY

Winks at JOE.

Sure, Larry ain't de on'y wise guy in dis dump, hey, Joe?

At a sound from the hall he turns as DON PARRITT *appears in the door-way.* ROCKY *speaks to* LARRY *out of the side of his mouth.*

Here's your guy.

PARRITT *comes forward. He is eighteen, tall and broad-shouldered but thin, gangling and awkward. His face is good-looking, with blond curly hair and large regular features, but his personality is unpleasant. There is a shifting defiance and ingratiation in his light-blue eyes and an irritating aggressiveness in his manner. His clothes and shoes are new, comparatively expensive, sporty in style. He looks as though he belonged in a pool room patronized by would-be sports. He glances around defensively, sees* LARRY *and comes forward.*

PARRITT
Hello, Larry.
He nods to ROCKY *and* JOE.
Hello.
They nod and size him up with expressionless eyes.

LARRY
Without cordiality.
What's up? I thought you'd be asleep.

PARRITT
Couldn't make it. I got sick of lying awake. Thought I might as well see if you were around.

LARRY
Indicates the chair on the right of table.
Sit down and join the bums then.
PARRITT *sits down.* LARRY *adds meaningfully.*
The rules of the house are that drinks may be served at all hours.

PARRITT
Forcing a smile.
I get you. But, hell, I'm just about broke.
He catches ROCKY's *and* JOE's *contemptuous glances—quickly.*
Oh, I know you guys saw— You think I've got a roll. Well, you're all wrong. I'll show you.

He takes a small wad of dollar bills from his pocket.

It's all ones. And I've got to live on it till I get a job.

Then with defensive truculence.

You think I fixed up a phony, don't you? Why the hell would I? Where would I get a real roll? You don't get rich doing what I've been doing. Ask Larry. You're lucky in the Movement if you have enough to eat.

LARRY *regards him puzzledly.*

ROCKY

Coldly.

What's de song and dance about? We ain't said nuttin'.

PARRITT

Lamely—placating them now.

Why, I was just putting you right. But I don't want you to think I'm a tightwad. I'll buy a drink if you want one.

JOE

Cheering up.

If? Man, when I don't want a drink, you call de morgue, tell dem come take Joe's body away, 'cause he's sure enuf dead. Gimme de bottle quick, Rocky, before he changes his mind!

ROCKY *passes him the bottle and glass. He pours a brimful drink and tosses it down his throat, and hands the bottle and glass to* LARRY.

ROCKY

I'll take a cigar when I go in de bar. What're you havin'?

PARRITT

Nothing. I'm on the wagon. What's the damage?

He holds out a dollar bill.

ROCKY

Fifteen cents.

He makes change from his pocket.

PARRITT

Must be some booze!

LARRY

It's cyanide cut with carbolic acid to give it a mellow flavor. Here's luck!

He drinks.

ROCKY

Guess I'll get back in de bar and catch a coupla winks before opening-up time.

He squeezes through the tables and disappears, right-rear, behind the curtain. In the section of bar at right, he comes forward and sits at the table and slumps back, closing his eyes and yawning.

JOE

Stares calculatingly at PARRITT *and then looks away—aloud to himself, philosophically.*

One-drink guy. Dat well done run dry. No hope till Harry's birthday party. 'Less Hickey shows up.

He turns to LARRY.

If Hickey comes, Larry, you wake me up if you has to bat me wid a chair.

He settles himself and immediately falls asleep.

PARRITT

Who's Hickey?

LARRY

A hardware drummer. An old friend of Harry Hope's and all the gang. He's a grand guy. He comes here twice a year regularly on a periodical drunk and blows in all his money.

PARRITT

With a disparaging glance around.

Must be hard up for a place to hang out.

LARRY

It has its points for him. He never runs into anyone he knows in his business here.

PARRITT

Lowering his voice.

Yes, that's what I want, too. I've got to stay under cover, Larry, like I told you last night.

LARRY
You did a lot of hinting. You didn't tell me anything.

PARRITT
You can guess, can't you?
He changes the subject abruptly.
I've been in some dumps on the Coast, but this is the limit. What kind of joint is it, anyway?

LARRY
With a sardonic grin.
What is it? It's the No Chance Saloon. It's Bedrock Bar, The End of the Line Café, The Bottom of the Sea Rathskeller! Don't you notice the beautiful calm in the atmosphere? That's because it's the last harbor. No one here has to worry about where they're going next, because there is no farther they can go. It's a great comfort to them. Although even here they keep up the appearances of life with a few harmless pipe dreams about their yesterdays and tomorrows, as you'll see for yourself if you're here long.

PARRITT
Stares at him curiously.
What's your pipe dream, Larry?

LARRY
Hiding resentment.
Oh, I'm the exception. I haven't any left, thank God.
Shortly.
Don't complain about this place. You couldn't find a better for lying low.

PARRITT
I'm glad of that, Larry. I don't feel any too damned good. I was knocked off my base by that business on the Coast, and since then it's been no fun dodging around the country, thinking every guy you see might be a dick.

LARRY

Sympathetically now.

No, it wouldn't be. But you're safe here. The cops ignore this dump.
They think it's as harmless as a graveyard.

He grins sardonically.

And, be God, they're right.

PARRITT

It's been lonely as hell.

Impulsively.

Christ, Larry, I was glad to find you. I kept saying to myself, "If I
can only find Larry. He's the one guy in the world who can understand—"

He hesitates, staring at LARRY *with a strange appeal.*

LARRY

Watching him puzzledly.

Understand what?

PARRITT

Hastily.

Why, all I've been through.

Looking away.

Oh, I know you're thinking. This guy has a hell of a nerve. I haven't
seen him since he was a kid. I'd forgotten he was alive. But I've never
forgotten you, Larry. You were the only friend of Mother's who ever
paid attention to me, or knew I was alive. All the others were too
busy with the Movement. Even Mother. And I had no Old Man. You
used to take me on your knee and tell me stories and crack jokes and
make me laugh. You'd ask me questions and take what I said seriously. I guess I got to feel in the years you lived with us that you'd
taken the place of my Old Man.

Embarrassedly.

But, hell, that sounds like a lot of mush. I suppose you don't remember a damned thing about it.

LARRY

Moved in spite of himself.

I remember well. You were a serious lonely little shaver.

Then resenting being moved, changes the subject.
How is it they didn't pick you up when they got your mother and the rest?

PARRITT
In a lowered voice but eagerly, as if he wanted this chance to tell about it.
I wasn't around, and as soon as I heard the news I went under cover. You've noticed my glad rags. I was staked to them—as a disguise, sort of. I hung around pool rooms and gambling joints and hooker shops, where they'd never look for a Wobblie, pretending I was a sport. Anyway, they'd grabbed everyone important, so I suppose they didn't think of me until afterward.

LARRY
The papers say the cops got them all dead to rights, that the Burns dicks knew every move before it was made, and someone inside the Movement must have sold out and tipped them off.

PARRITT
Turns to look LARRY *in the eyes—slowly.*
Yes, I guess that must be true, Larry. It hasn't come out who it was. It may never come out. I suppose whoever it was made a bargain with the Burns men to keep him out of it. They won't need his evidence.

LARRY
Tensely.
By God, I hate to believe it of any of the crowd, if I am through long since with any connection with them. I know they're damned fools, most of them, as stupidly greedy for power as the worst capitalist they attack, but I'd swear there couldn't be a yellow stool pigeon among them.

PARRITT
Sure. I'd have sworn that, too, Larry.

LARRY
I hope his soul rots in hell, whoever it is!

PARRITT
Yes, so do I.

LARRY
After a pause—shortly.
How did you locate me? I hoped I'd found a place of retirement here where no one in the Movement would ever come to disturb my peace.

PARRITT
I found out through Mother.

LARRY
I asked her not to tell anyone.

PARRITT
She didn't tell me, but she'd kept all your letters and I found where she'd hidden them in the flat. I sneaked up there one night after she was arrested.

LARRY
I'd never have thought she was a woman who'd keep letters.

PARRITT
No, I wouldn't, either. There's nothing soft or sentimental about Mother.

LARRY
I never answered her last letters. I haven't written her in a couple of years—or anyone else. I've gotten beyond the desire to communicate with the world—or, what's more to the point, let it bother me any more with its greedy madness.

PARRITT
It's funny Mother kept in touch with you so long. When she's finished with anyone, she's finished. She's always been proud of that. And you know how she feels about the Movement. Like a revivalist preacher about religion. Anyone who loses faith in it is more than dead to her; he's a Judas who ought to be boiled in oil. Yet she seemed to forgive you.

LARRY
Sardonically.

She didn't, don't worry. She wrote to denounce me and try to bring the sinner to repentance and a belief in the One True Faith again.

PARRITT

What made you leave the Movement, Larry? Was it on account of Mother?

LARRY
Starts.
Don't be a damned fool! What the hell put that in your head?

PARRITT

Why, nothing—except I remember what a fight you had with her before you left.

LARRY
Resentfully.
Well, if you do, I don't. That was eleven years ago. You were only seven. If we did quarrel, it was because I told her I'd become convinced the Movement was only a beautiful pipe dream.

PARRITT
With a strange smile.
I don't remember it that way.

LARRY

Then you can blame your imagination—and forget it.
He changes the subject abruptly.
You asked me why I quit the Movement. I had a lot of good reasons. One was myself, and another was my comrades, and the last was the breed of swine called men in general. For myself, I was forced to admit, at the end of thirty years' devotion to the Cause, that I was never made for it. I was born condemned to be one of those who has to see all sides of a question. When you're damned like that, the questions multiply for you until in the end it's all question and no answer. As history proves, to be a worldly success at anything, especially revolution, you have to wear blinders like a horse and see only straight in front of you. You have to see, too, that this is all black, and that is all white. As for my comrades in the Great Cause, I felt as Horace Walpole did about England, that he could love it if it weren't

for the people in it. The material the ideal free society must be constructed from is men themselves and you can't build a marble temple out of a mixture of mud and manure. When man's soul isn't a sow's ear, it will be time enough to dream of silk purses.

He chuckles sardonically—then irritably as if suddenly provoked at himself for talking so much.

Well, that's why I quit the Movement, if it leaves you any wiser. At any rate, you see it had nothing to do with your mother.

PARRITT

Smiles almost mockingly.

Oh, sure, I see. But I'll bet Mother has always thought it was on her account. You know her, Larry. To hear her go on sometimes, you'd think she was the Movement.

LARRY

Stares at him, puzzled and repelled—sharply.

That's a hell of a way for you to talk, after what happened to her!

PARRITT

At once confused and guilty.

Don't get me wrong. I wasn't sneering, Larry. Only kidding. I've said the same thing to her lots of times to kid her. But you're right. I know I shouldn't now. I keep forgetting she's in jail. It doesn't seem real. I can't believe it about her. She's always been so free. I— But I don't want to think of it.

LARRY *is moved to a puzzled pity in spite of himself.* PARRITT *changes the subject.*

What have you been doing all the years since you left—the Coast, Larry?

LARRY

Sardonically.

Nothing I could help doing. If I don't believe in the Movement, I don't believe in anything else either, especially not the State. I've refused to become a useful member of its society. I've been a philosophical drunken bum, and proud of it.

Abruptly his tone sharpens with resentful warning.

Listen to me. I hope you've deduced that I've my own reason for answering the impertinent questions of a stranger, for that's all you are to me. I have a strong hunch you've come here expecting something of me. I'm warning you, at the start, so there'll be no misunderstanding, that I've nothing left to give, and I want to be left alone, and I'll thank you to keep your life to yourself. I feel you're looking for some answer to something. I have no answer to give anyone, not even myself. Unless you can call what Heine wrote in his poem to morphine an answer.

He quotes a translation of the closing couplet sardonically.

"Lo, sleep is good; better is death; in sooth,
The best of all were never to be born."

PARRITT

Shrinks a bit frightenedly.

That's the hell of an answer.

Then a forced grin of bravado.

Still, you never know when it might come in handy.

He looks away. LARRY *stares at him puzzledly, interested in spite of himself and at the same time vaguely uneasy.*

LARRY

Forcing a casual tone.

I don't suppose you've had much chance to hear news of your mother since she's been in jail?

PARRITT

No. No chance.

He hesitates—then blurts out.

Anyway, I don't think she wants to hear from me. We had a fight just before that business happened. She bawled me out because I was going around with tarts. That got my goat, coming from her. I told her, "You've always acted the free woman, you've never let anything stop you from—"

He checks himself—goes on hurriedly.

That made her sore. She said she wouldn't give a damn what I did except she'd begun to suspect I was too interested in outside things and losing interest in the Movement.

LARRY
Stares at him.
And were you?

PARRITT
Hesitates — then with intensity.
Sure I was! I'm no damned fool! I couldn't go on believing forever
that gang was going to change the world by shooting off their loud
traps on soapboxes and sneaking around blowing up a lousy building
or a bridge! I got wise it was all a crazy pipe dream!
Appealingly.
The same as you did, Larry. That's why I came to you. I knew you'd
understand. What finished me was this last business of someone selling out. How can you believe anything after a thing like that happens? It knocks you cold! You don't know what the hell is what!
You're through!
Appealingly.
You know how I feel, don't you, Larry?
LARRY *stares at him, moved by sympathy and pity in spite of himself,
disturbed, and resentful at being disturbed, and puzzled by something
he feels about* PARRITT *that isn't right. But before he can reply,* HUGO
*suddenly raises his head from his arms in a half-awake alcoholic daze
and speaks.*

HUGO
Quotes aloud to himself in a guttural declamatory style.
"The days grow hot, O Babylon! 'Tis cool beneath thy villow trees!"
PARRITT *turns startledly as* HUGO *peers muzzily without recognition
at him.* HUGO *exclaims automatically in his tone of denunciation.*
Gottammed stool pigeon!

PARRITT
Shrinks away — stammers.
What? Who do you mean?
Then furiously.
You lousy bum, you can't call me that!
He draws back his fist.

HUGO

Ignores this—recognizing him now, bursts into his childish teasing giggle.

Hello, leedle Don! Leedle monkey-face. I did not recognize you. You have grown big boy. How is your mother? Where you come from?

He breaks into his wheedling, bullying tone.

Don't be a fool! Loan me a dollar! Buy me a trink!

As if this exhausted him, he abruptly forgets it and plumps his head down on his arms again and is asleep.

PARRITT

With eager relief.

Sure, I'll buy you a drink, Hugo. I'm broke, but I can afford one for you. I'm sorry I got sore. I ought to have remembered when you're soused you call everyone a stool pigeon. But it's no damned joke right at this time.

He turns to LARRY, *who is regarding him now fixedly with an uneasy expression as if he suddenly were afraid of his own thoughts—forcing a smile.*

Gee, he's passed out again.

He stiffens defensively.

What are you giving me the hard look for? Oh, I know. You thought I was going to hit him? What do you think I am? I've always had a lot of respect for Hugo. I've always stood up for him when people in the Movement panned him for an old drunken has-been. He had the guts to serve ten years in the can in his own country and get his eyes ruined in solitary. I'd like to see some of them here stick that. Well, they'll get a chance now to show—

Hastily.

I don't mean— But let's forget that. Tell me some more about this dump. Who are all these tanks? Who's that guy trying to catch pneumonia?

He indicates LEWIS.

LARRY

Stares at him almost frightenedly—then looks away and grasps eagerly this chance to change the subject. He begins to describe the sleepers with sardonic relish but at the same time showing his affection for them.

That's Captain Lewis, a one-time hero of the British Army. He strips to display that scar on his back he got from a native spear whenever he's completely plastered. The bewhiskered bloke opposite him is General Wetjoen, who led a commando in the War. The two of them met when they came here to work in the Boer War spectacle at the St. Louis Fair and they've been bosom pals ever since. They dream the hours away in happy dispute over the brave days in South Africa when they tried to murder each other. The little guy between them was in it, too, as correspondent for some English paper. His nickname here is Jimmy Tomorrow. He's the leader of our Tomorrow Movement.

PARRITT

What do they do for a living?

LARRY

As little as possible. Once in a while one of them makes a successful touch somewhere, and some of them get a few dollars a month from connections at home who pay it on condition they never come back. For the rest, they live on free lunch and their old friend, Harry Hope, who doesn't give a damn what anyone does or doesn't do, as long as he likes you.

PARRITT

It must be a tough life.

LARRY

It's not. Don't waste your pity. They wouldn't thank you for it. They manage to get drunk, by hook or crook, and keep their pipe dreams, and that's all they ask of life. I've never known more contented men. It isn't often that men attain the true goal of their heart's desire. The same applies to Harry himself and his two cronies at the far table. He's so satisfied with life he's never set foot out of this place since his wife died twenty years ago. He has no need of the outside world at all. This place has a fine trade from the Market people across the street and the waterfront workers, so in spite of Harry's thirst and his generous heart, he comes out even. He never worries in hard times because there's always old friends from the days when he was a jitney Tammany politician, and a friendly brewery to tide him over.

Don't ask me what his two pals work at because they don't. Except at being his lifetime guests. The one facing this way is his brother-in-law, Ed Mosher, who once worked for a circus in the ticket wagon. Pat McGloin, the other one, was a police lieutenant back in the flush times of graft when everything went. But he got too greedy and when the usual reform investigation came he was caught red-handed and thrown off the Force.

He nods at JOE.

Joe here has a yesterday in the same flush period. He ran a colored gambling house then and was a hell of a sport, so they say. Well, that's our whole family circle of inmates, except the two barkeeps and their girls, three ladies of the pavement that room on the third floor.

PARRITT

Bitterly.

To hell with them! I never want to see a whore again!

As LARRY *flashes him a puzzled glance, he adds confusedly.*

I mean, they always get you in dutch.

While he is speaking WILLIE OBAN *has opened his eyes. He leans toward them, drunk now from the effect of the huge drink he took, and speaks with a mocking suavity.*

WILLIE

Why omit me from your Who's Who in Dypsomania, Larry? An unpardonable slight, especially as I am the only inmate of royal blood.

To PARRITT—*ramblingly.*

Educated at Harvard, too. You must have noticed the atmosphere of culture here. My humble contribution. Yes, Generous Stranger—I trust you're generous—I was born in the purple, the son, but unfortunately not the heir, of the late world-famous Bill Oban, King of the Bucket Shops. A revolution deposed him, conducted by the District Attorney. He was sent into exile. In fact, not to mince matters, they locked him in the can and threw away the key. Alas, his was an adventurous spirit that pined in confinement. And so he died. Forgive these reminiscences. Undoubtedly all this is well known to you. Everyone in the world knows.

PARRITT

Uncomfortably.

Tough luck. No, I never heard of him.

WILLIE

Blinks at him incredulously.

Never heard? I thought everyone in the world— Why, even at Harvard I discovered my father was well known by reputation, although that was some time before the District Attorney gave him so much unwelcome publicity. Yes, even as a freshman I was notorious. I was accepted socially with all the warm cordiality that Henry Wadsworth Longfellow would have shown a drunken Negress dancing the can can at high noon on Brattle Street. Harvard was my father's idea. He was an ambitious man. Dictatorial, too. Always knowing what was best for me. But I did make myself a brilliant student. A dirty trick on my classmates, inspired by revenge, I fear.

He quotes.

"Dear college days, with pleasure rife! The grandest gladdest days of life!" But, of course, that is a Yale hymn, and they're given to rah-rah exaggeration at New Haven. I was a brilliant student at Law School, too. My father wanted a lawyer in the family. He was a calculating man. A thorough knowledge of the law close at hand in the house to help him find fresh ways to evade it. But I discovered the loophole of whiskey and escaped his jurisdiction.

Abruptly to PARRITT.

Speaking of whiskey, sir, reminds me—and, I hope, reminds you—that when meeting a Prince the customary salutation is "What'll you have?"

PARRITT

With defensive resentment.

Nix! All you guys seem to think I'm made of dough. Where would I get the coin to blow everyone?

WILLIE

Sceptically.

Broke? You haven't the thirsty look of the impecunious. I'd judge you to be a plutocrat, your pockets stuffed with ill-gotten gains. Two or three dollars, at least. And don't think we will question how you got it. As Vespasian remarked, the smell of all whiskey is sweet.

PARRITT

What do you mean, how I got it?

To LARRY, *forcing a laugh.*

It's a laugh, calling me a plutocrat, isn't it, Larry, when I've been in the Movement all my life.

LARRY *gives him an uneasy suspicious glance, then looks away, as if avoiding something he does not wish to see.*

WILLIE

Disgustedly.

Ah, one of those, eh? I believe you now, all right! Go away and blow yourself up, that's a good lad. Hugo is the only licensed preacher of that gospel here. A dangerous terrorist, Hugo! He would as soon blow the collar off a schooner of beer as look at you!

To LARRY.

Let us ignore this useless youth, Larry. Let us join in prayer that Hickey, the Great Salesman, will soon arrive bringing the blessed bourgeois long green! Would that Hickey or Death would come! Meanwhile, I will sing a song. A beautiful old New England folk ballad which I picked up at Harvard amid the debris of education.

He sings in a boisterous baritone, rapping on the table with his knuckles at the indicated spots in the song.

Jack, oh, Jack, was a sailor lad

And he came to a tavern for gin.

He rapped and he rapped with a

Rap, rap, rap.

But never a soul seemed in.

The drunks at the tables stir. ROCKY *gets up from his chair in the bar and starts back for the entrance to the back room.* HOPE *cocks one irritable eye over his specs.* JOE MOTT *opens both of his and grins.* WILLIE *interposes some drunken whimsical exposition to* LARRY.

The origin of this beautiful ditty is veiled in mystery, Larry. There was a legend bruited about in Cambridge lavatories that Waldo Emerson composed it during his uninformative period as a minister, while he was trying to write a sermon. But my own opinion is, it goes back much further, and Jonathan Edwards was the author of both words and music.

He sings.

> He rapped and rapped, and tapped and tapped
> Enough to wake the dead
> Till he heard a damsel
> *Rap, rap, rap.*
> On a window right over his head.

The drunks are blinking their eyes now, grumbling and cursing. ROCKY *appears from the bar at rear, right, yawning.*

HOPE

With fuming irritation.

Rocky! Bejees, can't you keep that crazy bastard quiet?

ROCKY *starts for* WILLIE.

WILLIE

And now the influence of a good woman enters our mariner's life. Well, perhaps "good" isn't the word. But very, very kind.

He sings.

> "Oh, come up," she cried, "my sailor lad,
> and you and I'll agree,
> And I'll show you the prettiest
> *Rap, rap, rap.*
> That ever you did see."

He speaks.

You see, Larry? The lewd Puritan touch, obviously, and it grows more marked as we go on.

He sings.

> Oh, he put his arm around her waist,
> He gazed in her bright blue eyes
> And then he—

But here ROCKY *shakes him roughly by the shoulder.*

ROCKY

Piano! What d'yuh tink dis dump is, a dump?

HOPE

Give him the bum's rush upstairs! Lock him in his room!

ROCKY
Yanks WILLIE *by the arm.*
Come on, Bum.

WILLIE
Dissolves into pitiable terror.
No! Please, Rocky! I'll go crazy up in that room alone! It's haunted!
I—
He calls to HOPE.
Please, Harry! Let me stay here! I'll be quiet!

HOPE
Immediately relents—indignantly.
What the hell you doing to him, Rocky? I didn't tell you to beat up
the poor guy. Leave him alone, long as he's quiet.
ROCKY *lets go of* WILLIE *disgustedly and goes back to his chair in the
bar.*

WILLIE
Huskily.
Thanks, Harry. You're a good scout.
*He closes his eyes and sinks back in his chair exhaustedly, twitching and
quivering again.*

HOPE
Addressing MCGLOIN *and* MOSHER, *who are sleepily awake—accusingly.*
Always the way. Can't trust nobody. Leave it to that Dago to keep
order and it's like bedlam in a cathouse, singing and everything. And
you two big barflies are a hell of a help to me, ain't you? Eat and sleep
and get drunk! All you're good for, bejees! Well, you can take that
"I'll-have-the-same" look off your maps! There ain't going to be no
more drinks on the house till hell freezes over!
*Neither of the two is impressed either by his insults or his threats. They
grin hangover grins of tolerant affection at him and wink at each other.*
HARRY *fumes.*
Yeah, grin! Wink, bejees! Fine pair of sons of bitches to have glued
on me for life!
But he can't get a rise out of them and he subsides into a fuming mumble.

Meanwhile, at the middle table, CAPTAIN LEWIS *and* GENERAL WETJOEN *are as wide awake as heavy hangovers permit.* JIMMY TOMORROW *nods, his eyes blinking.* LEWIS *is gazing across the table at* JOE MOTT, *who is still chuckling to himself over* WILLIE'S *song. The expression on* LEWIS'S *face is that of one who can't believe his eyes.*

LEWIS
Aloud to himself, with a muzzy wonder.
Good God! Have I been drinking at the same table with a bloody Kaffir?

JOE
Grinning.
Hello, Captain. You comin' up for air? Kaffir? Who's he?

WETJOEN
Blurrily.
Kaffir, dot's a nigger, Joe.
JOE *stiffens and his eyes narrow.* WETJOEN *goes on with heavy jocosity.*
Dot's joke on him, Joe. He don't know you. He's still plind drunk, the ploody Limey chentleman! A great mistake I missed him at the pattle of Modder River. Vit mine rifle I shoot damn fool Limey officers py the dozen, but him I miss. De pity of it!
He chuckles and slaps LEWIS *on his bare shoulder.*
Hey, wake up, Cecil, you ploody fool! Don't you know your old friend, Joe? He's no damned Kaffir! He's white, Joe is!

LEWIS
Light dawning—contritely.
My profound apologies, Joseph, old chum. Eyesight a trifle blurry, I'm afraid. Whitest colored man I ever knew. Proud to call you my friend. No hard feelings, what?
He holds out his hand.

JOE
At once grins good-naturedly and shakes his hand.
No, Captain, I know it's mistake. Youse regular, if you is a Limey.
Then his face hardening.
But I don't stand for "nigger" from nobody. Never did. In de old

days, people calls me "nigger" wakes up in de hospital. I was de leader ob de Dirty Half-Dozen Gang. All six of us colored boys, we was tough and I was de toughest.

WETJOEN
Inspired to boastful reminiscence.
Me, in old days in Transvaal, I vas so tough and strong I grab axle of ox wagon mit full load and lift like feather.

LEWIS
Smiling amiably.
As for you, my balmy Boer that walks like a man, I say again it was a grave error in our foreign policy ever to set you free, once we nabbed you and your commando with Cronje. We should have taken you to the London zoo and incarcerated you in the baboons' cage. With a sign: "Spectators may distinguish the true baboon by his blue behind."

WETJOEN
Grins.
Gott! To dink, ten better Limey officers, at least, I shoot clean in the mittle of forehead at Spion Kopje, and you I miss! I neffer forgive myself!

JIMMY TOMORROW *blinks benignantly from one to the other with a gentle drunken smile.*

JIMMY
Sentimentally.
Now, come, Cecil, Piet! We must forget the War. Boer and Briton, each fought fairly and played the game till the better man won and then we shook hands. We are all brothers within the Empire united beneath the flag on which the sun never sets.
Tears come to his eyes. He quotes with great sentiment, if with slight application.
"Ship me somewhere east of Suez—"

LARRY
Breaks in sardonically.
Be God, you're there already, Jimmy. Worst is best here, and East is West, and tomorrow is yesterday. What more do you want?

JIMMY

With bleery benevolence, shaking his head in mild rebuke.

No, Larry, old friend, you can't deceive me. You pretend a bitter, cynic philosophy, but in your heart you are the kindest man among us.

LARRY

Disconcerted—irritably.

The hell you say!

PARRITT

Leans toward him—confidentially.

What a bunch of cuckoos!

JIMMY

As if reminded of something—with a pathetic attempt at a brisk, no-more-nonsense air.

Tomorrow, yes. It's high time I straightened out and got down to business again.

He brushes his sleeve fastidiously.

I must have this suit cleaned and pressed. I can't look like a tramp when I—

JOE

Who has been brooding—interrupts.

Yes, suh, white folks always said I was white. In de days when I was flush, Joe Mott's de only colored man dey allows in de white gamblin' houses. "You're all right, Joe, you're white," dey says.

He chuckles.

Wouldn't let me play craps, dough. Dey know I could make dem dice behave. "Any odder game and any limit you like, Joe," dey says. Man, de money I lost!

He chuckles—then with an underlying defensiveness.

Look at de Big Chief in dem days. He knew I was white. I'd saved my dough so I could start my own gamblin' house. Folks in de know tells me, see de man at de top, den you never has trouble. You git Harry Hope give you a letter to de Chief. And Harry does. Don't you, Harry?

HOPE

Preoccupied with his own thought.

Eh? Sure. Big Bill was a good friend of mine. I had plenty of friends high up in those days. Still could have if I wanted to go out and see them. Sure, I gave you a letter. I said you was white. What the hell of it?

JOE

To CAPTAIN LEWIS *who has relapsed into a sleepy daze and is listening to him with an absurd strained attention without comprehending a word.*

Dere. You see, Captain. I went to see de Chief, shakin' in my boots, and dere he is sittin' behind a big desk, lookin' as big as a freight train. He don't look up. He keeps me waitin' and waitin', and after 'bout an hour, seems like to me, he says slow and quiet like dere wasn't no harm in him, "You want to open a gamblin' joint, does you, Joe?" But he don't give me no time to answer. He jumps up, lookin' as big as two freight trains, and he pounds his fist like a ham on de desk, and he shouts, "You black son of a bitch, Harry says you're white and you better be white or dere's a little iron room up de river waitin' for you!" Den he sits down and says quiet again, "All right. You can open. Git de hell outa here!" So I opens, and he finds out I'se white, sure 'nuff, 'cause I run wide open for years and pays my sugar on de dot, and de cops and I is friends.

He chuckles with pride.

Dem old days! Many's de night I come in here. Dis was a first-class hangout for sports in dem days. Good whiskey, fifteen cents, two for two bits. I t'rows down a fifty-dollar bill like it was trash paper and says, "Drink it up, boys, I don't want no change." Ain't dat right, Harry?

HOPE

Caustically.

Yes, and bejees, if I ever seen you throw fifty cents on the bar now, I'd know I had delirium tremens! You've told that story ten million times and if I have to hear it again, that'll give me D.T.s anyway!

JOE
Chuckling.
Gittin' drunk every day for twenty years ain't give you de Brooklyn boys. You needn't be scared of me!

LEWIS
Suddenly turns and beams on HOPE.
Thank you, Harry, old chum. I will have a drink, now you mention it, seeing it's so near your birthday.
The others laugh.

HOPE
Puts his hand to his ear—angrily.
What's that? I can't hear you.

LEWIS
Sadly.
No, I fancied you wouldn't.

HOPE
I don't have to hear, bejees! Booze is the only thing you ever talk about!

LEWIS
Sadly.
True. Yet there was a time when my conversation was more comprehensive. But as I became burdened with years, it seemed rather pointless to discuss my other subject.

HOPE
You can't joke with me! How much room rent do you owe me, tell me that?

LEWIS
Sorry. Adding has always baffled me. Subtraction is my forte.

HOPE
Snarling.
Arrh! Think you're funny! Captain, bejees! Showing off your wounds! Put on your clothes, for Christ's sake! This ain't no Turk-

44

ish bath! Lousy Limey army! Took 'em years to lick a gang of Dutch hayseeds!

WETJOEN
Dot's right, Harry. Gif him hell!

HOPE
No lip out of you, neither, you Dutch spinach! General, hell! Salvation Army, that's what you'd ought t'been General in! Bragging what a shot you were, and, bejees, you missed him! And he missed you, that's just as bad! And now the two of you bum on me!
Threateningly.
But you've broke the camel's back this time, bejees! You pay up tomorrow or out you go!

LEWIS
Earnestly.
My dear fellow, I give you my word of honor as an officer and a gentleman, you shall be paid tomorrow.

WETJOEN
Ve swear it, Harry! Tomorrow vidout fail!

MCGLOIN
A twinkle in his eye.
There you are, Harry. Sure, what could be fairer?

MOSHER
With a wink at MCGLOIN.
Yes, you can't ask more than that, Harry. A promise is a promise—as I've often discovered.

HOPE
Turns on them.
I mean the both of you, too! An old grafting flatfoot and a circus bunco steerer! Fine company for me, bejees! Couple of con men living in my flat since Christ knows when! Getting fat as hogs, too! And you ain't even got the decency to get me upstairs where I got a good bed! Let me sleep on a chair like a bum! Kept me down here waitin' for Hickey to show up, hoping I'd blow you to more drinks!

MCGLOIN

Ed and I did our damnedest to get you up, didn't we, Ed?

MOSHER

We did. But you said you couldn't bear the flat because it was one of those nights when memory brought poor old Bessie back to you.

HOPE

His face instantly becoming long and sad and sentimental—mournfully.
Yes, that's right, boys. I remember now. I could almost see her in every room just as she used to be—and it's twenty years since she— *His throat and eyes fill up. A suitable sentimental hush falls on the room.*

LARRY

In a sardonic whisper to PARRITT.
Isn't a pipe dream of yesterday a touching thing? By all accounts, Bessie nagged the hell out of him.

JIMMY

Who has been dreaming, a look of prim resolution on his face, speaks aloud to himself.
No more of this sitting around and loafing. Time I took hold of myself. I must have my shoes soled and heeled and shined first thing tomorrow morning. A general spruce-up. I want to have a well-groomed appearance when I—
His voice fades out as he stares in front of him. No one pays any attention to him except LARRY *and* PARRITT.

LARRY

As before, in a sardonic aside to PARRITT.
The tomorrow movement is a sad and beautiful thing, too!

MCGLOIN

With a huge sentimental sigh—and a calculating look at HOPE.
Poor old Bessie! You don't find her like in these days. A sweeter woman never drew breath.

MOSHER

In a similar calculating mood.

Good old Bess. A man couldn't want a better sister than she was to me.

HOPE
Mournfully.
Twenty years, and I've never set foot out of this house since the day I buried her. Didn't have the heart. Once she'd gone, I didn't give a damn for anything. I lost all my ambition. Without her, nothing seemed worth the trouble. You remember, Ed, you, too, Mac—the boys was going to nominate me for Alderman. It was all fixed. Bessie wanted it and she was so proud. But when she was taken, I told them, "No, boys, I can't do it. I simply haven't the heart. I'm through." I would have won the election easy, too.
He says this a bit defiantly.
Oh, I know there was jealous wise guys said the boys was giving me the nomination because they knew they couldn't win that year in this ward. But that's a damned lie! I knew every man, woman and child in the ward, almost. Bessie made me make friends with everyone, helped me remember all their names. I'd have been elected easy.

MCGLOIN
You would, Harry. It was a sure thing.

MOSHER
A dead cinch, Harry. Everyone knows that.

HOPE
Sure they do. But after Bessie died, I didn't have the heart. Still, I know while she'd appreciate my grief, she wouldn't want it to keep me cooped up in here all my life. So I've made up my mind I'll go out soon. Take a walk around the ward, see all the friends I used to know, get together with the boys and maybe tell 'em I'll let 'em deal me a hand in their game again. Yes, bejees, I'll do it. My birthday, tomorrow, that'd be the right time to turn over a new leaf. Sixty. That ain't too old.

MCGLOIN
Flatteringly.
It's the prime of life, Harry.

MOSHER

Wonderful thing about you, Harry, you keep young as you ever was.

JIMMY

Dreaming aloud again.

Get my things from the laundry. They must still have them. Clean collar and shirt. If I wash the ones I've got on any more, they'll fall apart. Socks, too. I want to make a good appearance. I met Dick Trumbull on the street a year or two ago. He said, "Jimmy, the publicity department's never been the same since you got—resigned. It's dead as hell." I said, "I know. I've heard rumors the management were at their wits' end and would be only too glad to have me run it for them again. I think all I'd have to do would be go and see them and they'd offer me the position. Don't you think so, Dick?" He said, "Sure, they would, Jimmy. Only take my advice and wait a while until business conditions are better. Then you can strike them for a bigger salary than you got before, do you see?" I said, "Yes, I do see, Dick, and many thanks for the tip." Well, conditions must be better by this time. All I have to do is get fixed up with a decent front tomorrow, and it's as good as done.

HOPE

Glances at JIMMY *with a condescending affectionate pity—in a hushed voice.*

Poor Jimmy's off on his pipe dream again. Bejees, he takes the cake! *This is too much for* LARRY. *He cannot restrain a sardonic guffaw. But no one pays any attention to him.*

LEWIS

Opens his eyes, which are drowsing again—dreamily to WETJOEN.

I'm sorry we had to postpone our trip again this April, Piet. I hoped the blasted old estate would be settled up by then. The damned lawyers can't hold up the settlement much longer. We'll make it next year, even if we have to work and earn our passage money, eh? You'll stay with me at the old place as long as you like, then you can take the *Union Castle* from Southhampton to Cape Town.

Sentimentally, with real yearning.

England in April. I want you to see that, Piet. The old veldt has its points, I'll admit, but it isn't home—especially home in April.

WETJOEN
Blinks drowsily at him—dreamily.
Ja, Cecil, I know how beautiful it must be, from all you tell me many times. I vill enjoy it. But I shall enjoy more ven I am home, too. The veldt, ja! You could put England on it, and it would look like a farmer's small garden. Py Gott, there is space to be free, the air like vine is, you don't need booze to be drunk! My relations vill so surprised be. They vill not know me, it is so many years. Dey vill be so glad I haf come home at last.

JOE
Dreamily.
I'll make my stake and get my new gamblin' house open before you boys leave. You got to come to de openin'. I'll treat you white. If you're broke, I'll stake you to buck any game you chooses. If you wins, dat's velvet for you. If you loses, it don't count. Can't treat you no whiter dan dat, can I?

HOPE
Again with condescending pity.
Bejees, Jimmy's started them off smoking the same hop.
But the three are finished, their eyes closed again in sleep or a drowse.

LARRY
Aloud to himself—in his comically tense, crazy whisper.
Be God, this bughouse will drive me stark, raving loony yet!

HOPE
Turns on him with fuming suspicion.
What? What d'you say?

LARRY
Placatingly.
Nothing, Harry. I had a crazy thought in my head.

HOPE
Irascibly.

Crazy is right! Yah! The old wise guy! Wise, hell! A damned old fool Anarchist I-Won't-Worker! I'm sick of you and Hugo, too. Bejees, you'll pay up tomorrow, or I'll start a Harry Hope Revolution! I'll tie a dispossess bomb to your tails that'll blow you out in the street! Bejees, I'll make your Movement move!

The witticism delights him and he bursts into a shrill cackle. At once MCGLOIN *and* MOSHER *guffaw enthusiastically.*

MOSHER
Flatteringly.
Harry, you sure say the funniest things!
He reaches on the table as if he expected a glass to be there—then starts with well-acted surprise.
Hell, where's my drink? That Rocky is too damned fast cleaning tables. Why, I'd only taken one sip of it.

HOPE
His smiling face congealing.
No, you don't!
Acidly.
Any time you only take one sip of a drink, you'll have lockjaw and paralysis! Think you can kid me with those old circus con games?— me, that's known you since you was knee-high, and, bejees, you was a crook even then!

MCGLOIN
Grinning.
It's not like you to be so hard-hearted, Harry. Sure, it's hot, parching work laughing at your jokes so early in the morning on an empty stomach!

HOPE
Yah! You, Mac! Another crook! Who asked you to laugh? We was talking about poor old Bessie, and you and her no-good brother start to laugh! A hell of a thing! Talking mush about her, too! "Good old Bess." Bejees, she'd never forgive me if she knew I had you two bums living in her flat, throwing ashes and cigar butts on her carpet. You know her opinion of you, Mac. "That Pat McGloin is the biggest

drunken grafter that ever disgraced the police force," she used to say to me. "I hope they send him to Sing Sing for life."

MCGLOIN
Unperturbed.
She didn't mean it. She was angry at me because you used to get me drunk. But Bess had a heart of gold underneath her sharpness. She knew I was innocent of all the charges.

WILLIE
Jumps to his feet drunkenly and points a finger at MCGLOIN — *imitating the manner of a cross-examiner — coldly.*
One moment, please. Lieutenant McGloin! Are you aware you are under oath? Do you realize what the penalty for perjury is?
Purringly.
Come now, Lieutenant, isn't it a fact that you're as guilty as hell? No, don't say, "How about your old man?" I am asking the questions. The fact that he was a crooked old bucket-shop bastard has no bearing on your case.
With a change to maudlin joviality.
Gentlemen of the Jury, court will now recess while the D.A. sings out a little ditty he learned at Harvard. It was composed in a wanton moment by the Dean of the Divinity School on a moonlight night in July, 1776, while sobering up in a Turkish bath.
He sings.

"Oh, come up," she cried, "my sailor lad,
And you and I'll agree.
And I'll show you the prettiest
Rap, rap, rap on table.
That ever you did see."

Suddenly he catches HOPE'S *eyes fixed on him condemningly, and sees* ROCKY *appearing from the bar. He collapses back on his chair, pleading miserably.*
Please, Harry! I'll be quiet! Don't make Rocky bounce me upstairs! I'll go crazy alone!
To MCGLOIN.
I apologize, Mac. Don't get sore. I was only kidding you.
ROCKY, *at a relenting glance from* HOPE, *returns to the bar.*

MCGLOIN

Good-naturedly.

Sure, kid all you like, Willie. I'm hardened to it.

He pauses—seriously.

But I'm telling you some day before long I'm going to make them reopen my case. Everyone knows there was no real evidence against me, and I took the fall for the ones higher up. I'll be found innocent this time and reinstated.

Wistfully.

I'd like to have my old job on the Force back. The boys tell me there's fine pickings these days, and I'm not getting rich here, sitting with a parched throat waiting for Harry Hope to buy a drink.

He glances reproachfully at HOPE.

WILLIE

Of course, you'll be reinstated, Mac. All you need is a brilliant young attorney to handle your case. I'll be straightened out and on the wagon in a day or two. I've never practiced but I was one of the most brilliant students in Law School, and your case is just the opportunity I need to start.

Darkly.

Don't worry about my not forcing the D.A. to reopen your case. I went through my father's papers before the cops destroyed them, and I remember a lot of people, even if I can't prove—

Coaxingly.

You will let me take your case, won't you, Mac?

MCGLOIN

Soothingly.

Sure I will and it'll make your reputation, Willie.

MOSHER *winks at* HOPE, *shaking his head, and* HOPE *answers with identical pantomime, as though to say, "Poor dopes, they're off again!"*

LARRY

Aloud to himself more than to PARRITT—*with irritable wonder.*

Ah, be damned! Haven't I heard their visions a thousand times? Why should they get under my skin now? I've got the blues, I guess. I wish to hell Hickey'd turn up.

MOSHER

Calculatingly solicitous—whispering to HOPE.

Poor Willie needs a drink bad, Harry—and I think if we all joined him it'd make him feel he was among friends and cheer him up.

HOPE

More circus con tricks!

Scathingly.

You talking of your dear sister! Bessie had you sized up. She used to tell me, "I don't know what you can see in that worthless, drunken, petty-larceny brother of mine. If I had my way," she'd say, "he'd get booted out in the gutter on his fat behind." Sometimes she didn't say behind, either.

MOSHER

Grins genially.

Yes, dear old Bess had a quick temper, but there was no real harm in her.

He chuckles reminiscently.

Remember the time she sent me down to the bar to change a ten-dollar bill for her?

HOPE

Has to grin himself.

Bejees, do I! She coulda bit a piece out of a stove lid, after she found it out.

He cackles appreciatively.

MOSHER

I was sure surprised when she gave me the ten spot. Bess usually had better sense, but she was in a hurry to go to church. I didn't really mean to do it, but you know how habit gets you. Besides, I still worked then, and the circus season was going to begin soon, and I needed a little practice to keep my hand in. Or, you never can tell, the first rube that came to my wagon for a ticket might have left with the right change and I'd be disgraced.

He chuckles.

I said, "I'm sorry, Bess, but I had to take it all in dimes. Here, hold

out your hands and I'll count it out for you, so you won't kick afterwards I short-changed you."

He begins a count which grows more rapid as he goes on.

Ten, twenty, thirty, forty, fifty, sixty, seventy, eighty, ninety, a dollar. Ten, twenty, thirty, forty, fifty, sixty— You're counting with me,
Bess, aren't you?—eighty, ninety, two dollars. Ten, twenty— Those
are pretty shoes you got on, Bess—forty, fifty, seventy, eighty, ninety,
three dollars. Ten, twenty, thirty— What's on at the church tonight,
Bess?—fifty, sixty, seventy, ninety, four dollars. Ten, twenty, thirty,
fifty, seventy, eighty, ninety— That's a swell new hat, Bess, looks
very becoming—six dollars.

He chuckles.

And so on. I'm bum at it now for lack of practice, but in those days
I could have short-changed the Keeper of the Mint.

HOPE

Grinning.

Stung her for two dollars and a half, wasn't it, Ed?

MOSHER

Yes. A fine percentage, if I do say so, when you're dealing to someone
who's sober and can count. I'm sorry to say she discovered my mistakes in arithmetic just after I beat it around the corner. She counted
it over herself. Bess somehow never had the confidence in me a sister
should.

He sighs tenderly.

Dear old Bess.

HOPE

Indignant now.

You're a fine guy bragging how you short-changed your own sister!
Bejees, if there was a war and you was in it, they'd have to padlock
the pockets of the dead!

MOSHER

A bit hurt at this.

That's going pretty strong, Harry. I always gave a sucker some
chance. There wouldn't be no fun robbing the dead.

He becomes reminiscently melancholy.

Gosh, thinking of the old ticket wagon brings those days back. The greatest life on earth with the greatest show of earth! The grandest crowd of regular guys ever gathered under one tent! I'd sure like to shake their hands again!

HOPE
Acidly.
They'd have guns in theirs. They'd shoot you on sight. You've touched every damned one of them. Bejees, you've even borrowed fish from the trained seals and peanuts from every elephant that remembered you!
This fancy tickles him and he gives a cackling laugh.

MOSHER
Overlooking this—dreamily.
You know, Harry, I've made up my mind I'll see the boss in a couple of days and ask for my old job. I can get back my magic touch with change easy, and I can throw him a line of bull that'll kid him I won't be so unreasonable about sharing the profits next time.
With insinuating complaint.
There's no percentage in hanging around this dive, taking care of you and shooting away your snakes, when I don't even get an eye-opener for my trouble.

HOPE
Implacably.
No!

MOSHER *sighs and gives up and closes his eyes. The others, except* LARRY *and* PARRITT, *are all dozing again now.* HOPE *goes on grumbling.*
Go to hell or the circus, for all I care. Good riddance, bejees! I'm sick of you!
Then worriedly.
Say, Ed, what the hell you think's happened to Hickey? I hope he'll turn up. Always got a million funny stories. You and the other bums have begun to give me the graveyard fantods. I'd like a good laugh with old Hickey.
He chuckles at a memory.

Remember that gag he always pulls about his wife and the iceman?
He'd make a cat laugh!

ROCKY *appears from the bar. He comes front, behind* MOSHER'S *chair,
and begins pushing the black curtain along the rod to the rear wall.*

ROCKY
Openin' time, Boss.
*He presses a button at rear which switches off the lights. The back room
becomes drabber and dingier than ever in the gray daylight that comes
from the street windows, off right, and what light can penetrate the grime
of the two backyard windows at left.* ROCKY *turns back to* HOPE—
grumpily.
Why don't you go up to bed, Boss? Hickey'd never turn up dis time
of de mornin'!

HOPE
Starts and listens.
Someone's coming now.

ROCKY
Listens.
Aw, dat's on'y my two pigs. It's about time dey showed.
He goes back toward the door at left of the bar.

HOPE
Sourly disappointed.
You keep them dumb broads quiet. I don't want to go to bed. I'm
going to catch a couple more winks here and I don't want no damn-
fool laughing and screeching.
He settles himself in his chair, grumbling.
Never thought I'd see the day when Harry Hope's would have tarts
rooming in it. What'd Bessie think? But I don't let 'em use my rooms
for business. And they're good kids. Good as anyone else. They got
to make a living. Pay their rent, too, which is more than I can say
for—
He cocks an eye over his specs at MOSHER *and grins with satisfaction.*
Bejees, Ed, I'll bet Bessie is doing somersaults in her grave!
He chuckles. But MOSHER'S *eyes are closed, his head nodding, and he
doesn't reply, so* HOPE *closes his eyes.* ROCKY *has opened the barroom*

door at rear and is standing in the hall beyond it, facing right. A girl's laugh is heard.

ROCKY
Warningly.
Nix! Piano!
He comes in, beckoning them to follow. He goes behind the bar and gets a whiskey bottle and glasses and chairs. MARGIE *and* PEARL *follow him, casting a glance around. Everyone except* LARRY *and* PARRITT *is asleep or dozing. Even* PARRITT *has his eyes closed. The two girls, neither much over twenty, are typical dollar street walkers, dressed in the usual tawdry get-up.* PEARL *is obviously Italian with black hair and eyes.* MARGIE *has brown hair and hazel eyes, a slum New Yorker of mixed blood. Both are plump and have a certain prettiness that shows even through their blobby make-up. Each retains a vestige of youthful freshness, although the game is beginning to get them and give them hard, worn expressions. Both are sentimental, feather-brained, giggly, lazy, good-natured and reasonably contented with life. Their attitude toward* ROCKY *is much that of two maternal, affectionate sisters toward a bullying brother whom they like to tease and spoil. His attitude toward them is that of the owner of two performing pets he has trained to do a profitable act under his management. He feels a proud proprietor's affection for them, and is tolerantly lax in his discipline.*

MARGIE
Glancing around.
Jees, Poil, it's de Morgue wid all de stiffs on deck.
She catches LARRY's *eye and smiles affectionately.*
Hello, Old Wise Guy, ain't you died yet?

LARRY
Grinning.
Not yet, Margie. But I'm waiting impatiently for the end.
PARRITT *opens his eyes to look at the two girls, but as soon as they glance at him he closes them again and turns his head away.*

MARGIE
As she and PEARL *come to the table at right, front, followed by* ROCKY.
Who's de new guy? Friend of yours, Larry?

57

Automatically she smiles seductively at PARRITT *and addresses him in a professional chant.*
Wanta have a good time, kid?

PEARL
Aw, he's passed out. Hell wid him!

HOPE
Cocks an eye over his specs at them—with drowsy irritation.
You dumb broads cut the loud talk.
He shuts his eye again.

ROCKY
Admonishing them good-naturedly.
Sit down before I knock yuh down.
MARGIE *and* PEARL *sit at left, and rear, of table,* ROCKY *at right of it. The girls pour drinks.* ROCKY *begins in a brisk, business-like manner but in a lowered voice with an eye on* HOPE.
Well, how'd you tramps do?

MARGIE
Pretty good. Didn't we, Poil?

PEARL
Sure. We nailed a coupla all-night guys.

MARGIE
On Sixth Avenoo. Boobs from de sticks.

PEARL
Stinko, de bot' of 'em.

MARGIE
We thought we was in luck. We steered dem to a real hotel. We figgered dey was too stinko to bother us much and we could cop a good sleep in beds that ain't got cobble stones in de mattress like de ones in dis dump.

PEARL
But we was outa luck. Dey didn't bother us much dat way, but dey wouldn't go to sleep either, see? Jees, I never hoid such gabby guys.

MARGIE

Dey got onta politics, drinkin' outa de bottle. Dey forgot we was around. "De Bull Moosers is de on'y reg'lar guys," one guy says. And de other guy says, "You're a God-damned liar! And I'm a Republican!" Den dey'd laugh.

PEARL

Den dey'd get mad and make a bluff dey was goin' to scrap, and den dey'd make up and cry and sing "School Days." Jees, imagine tryin' to sleep wid dat on de phonograph!

MARGIE

Maybe you tink we wasn't glad when de house dick come up and told us all to git dressed and take de air!

PEARL

We told de guys we'd wait for dem 'round de corner.

MARGIE

So here we are.

ROCKY

Sententiously.

Yeah. I see you. But I don't see no dough yet.

PEARL

With a wink at MARGIE — *teasingly.*

Right on de job, ain't he, Margie?

MARGIE

Yeah, our little business man! Dat's him!

ROCKY

Come on! Dig!

They both pull up their skirts to get the money from their stockings. ROCKY *watches this move carefully.*

PEARL

Amused.

Pipe him keepin' cases, Margie.

MARGIE
Amused.
Scared we're holdin' out on him.

PEARL
Way he grabs, yuh'd tink it was him done de woik.
She holds out a little roll of bills to ROCKY.
Here y'are, Grafter!

MARGIE
Holding hers out.
We hope it chokes yuh.
ROCKY *counts the money quickly and shoves it in his pocket.*

ROCKY
Genially.
You dumb baby dolls gimme a pain. What would you do wid money if I wasn't around? Give it all to some pimp.

PEARL
Teasingly.
Jees, what's the difference —?
Hastily.
Aw, I don't mean dat, Rocky.

ROCKY
His eyes growing hard — slowly.
A lotta difference, get me?

PEARL
Don't get sore. Jees, can't yuh take a little kiddin'?

MARGIE
Sure, Rocky, Poil was on'y kiddin'.
Soothingly.
We know yuh got a reg'lar job. Dat's why we like yuh, see? Yuh don't live offa us. Yuh're a bartender.

ROCKY
Genially again.
Sure, I'm a bartender. Everyone knows me knows dat. And I treat

you goils right, don't I? Jees, I'm wise yuh hold out on me, but I know it ain't much, so what the hell, I let yuh get away wid it. I tink yuh're a coupla good kids. Yuh're aces wid me, see?

PEARL

You're aces wid us, too. Ain't he, Margie?

MARGIE

Sure, he's aces.

ROCKY *beams complacently and takes the glasses back to the bar.* MARGIE *whispers.*

Yuh sap, don't yuh know enough not to kid him on dat? Serve yuh right if he beat yuh up!

PEARL

Admiringly.

Jees, I'll bet he'd give yuh an awful beatin', too, once he started. Ginnies got awful tempers.

MARGIE

Anyway, we wouldn't keep no pimp, like we was reg'lar old whores. We ain't dat bad.

PEARL

No. We're tarts, but dat's all.

ROCKY

Rinsing glasses behind the bar.

Cora got back around three o'clock. She woke up Chuck and dragged him outa de hay to go to a chop suey joint.

Disgustedly.

Imagine him standin' for dat stuff!

MARGIE

Disgustedly.

I'll bet dey been sittin' around kiddin' demselves wid dat old pipe dream about getting' married and settlin' down on a farm. Jees, when Chuck's on de wagon, dey never lay off dat dope! Dey give yuh an earful every time yuh talk to 'em!

PEARL

Yeah. Chuck wid a silly grin on his ugly map, de big boob, and Cora gigglin' like she was in grammar school and some tough guy'd just told her babies wasn't brung down de chimney by a boid!

MARGIE

And her on de turf long before me and you was! And bot' of 'em arguin' all de time, Cora sayin' she's scared to marry him because he'll go on drunks again. Just as dough any drunk could scare Cora!

PEARL

And him swearin', de big liar, he'll never go on no more periodicals! An' den her pretendin'—But it gives me a pain to talk about it. We ought to phone de booby hatch to send round de wagon for 'em.

ROCKY

Comes back to the table—disgustedly.

Yeah, of all de pipe dreams in dis dump, dey got de nuttiest! And nuttin' stops dem. Dey been dreamin' it for years, every time Chuck goes on de wagon. I never could figger it. What would gettin' married get dem? But de farm stuff is de sappiest part. When bot' of 'em was dragged up in dis ward and ain't never been nearer a farm dan Coney Island! Jees, dey'd tink dey'd gone deef if dey didn't hear de El rattle! Dey'd get D.T.s if dey ever hoid a cricket choip! I hoid crickets once on my cousin's place in Joisey. I couldn't sleep a wink. Dey give me de heebie-jeebies.

With deeper disgust.

Jees, can yuh picture a good barkeep like Chuck diggin' spuds? And imagine a whore hustlin' de cows home! For Christ sake! Ain't dat a sweet picture!

MARGIE

Rebukingly.

Yuh oughtn't to call Cora dat, Rocky. She's a good kid. She may be a tart, but—

ROCKY

Considerately.

Sure, dat's all I meant, a tart.

PEARL

Giggling.

But he's right about de damned cows, Margie. Jees, I bet Cora don't know which end of de cow has de horns! I'm goin' to ask her.

There is the noise of a door opening in the hall and the sound of a man's and woman's arguing voices.

ROCKY

Here's your chance. Dat's dem two nuts now.

CORA *and* CHUCK *look in from the hallway and then come in.* CORA *is a thin peroxide blonde, a few years older than* PEARL *and* MARGIE, *dressed in similar style, her round face showing more of the wear and tear of her trade than theirs, but still with traces of a doll-like prettiness.* CHUCK *is a tough, thick-necked, barrel-chested Italian-American, with a fat, amiable, swarthy face. He has on a straw hat with a vivid band, a loud suit, tie and shirt, and yellow shoes. His eyes are clear and he looks healthy and strong as an ox.*

CORA

Gaily.

Hello, bums.

She looks around.

Jees, de Morgue on a rainy Sunday night!

She waves to LARRY—*affectionately.*

Hello, Old Wise Guy! Ain't you croaked yet?

LARRY

Grins.

Not yet, Cora. It' damned tiring, this waiting for the end.

CORA

Aw, gwan, you'll never die! Yuh'll have to hire someone to croak yuh wid an axe.

HOPE

Cocks one sleepy eye at her—irritably.

You dumb hookers, cut the loud noise! This ain't a cat-house!

CORA
Teasingly.
My, Harry! Such language!

HOPE
Closes his eyes—to himself with a gratified chuckle.
Bejees, I'll bet Bessie's turning over in her grave!
CORA *sits down between* MARGIE *and* PEARL. CHUCK *takes an empty chair from* HOPE's *table and puts it by hers and sits down. At* LARRY's *table,* PARRITT *is glaring resentfully toward the girls.*

PARRITT
If I'd known this dump was a hooker hangout, I'd never have come here.

LARRY
Watching him.
You seem down on the ladies.

PARRITT
Vindictively.
I hate every bitch that ever lived! They're all alike!
Catching himself guiltily.
You can understand how I feel, can't you, when it was getting mixed up with a tart that made me have that fight with Mother?
Then with a resentful sneer.
But what the hell does it matter to you? You're in the grandstand. You're through with life.

LARRY
Sharply.
I'm glad you remember it. I don't want to know a damned thing about your business.
He closes his eyes and settles on his chair as if preparing for sleep. PARRITT *stares at him sneeringly. Then he looks away and his expression becomes furtive and frightened.*

CORA
Who's de guy wid Larry?

ROCKY

A tightwad. To hell wid him.

PEARL

Say, Cora, wise me up. Which end of a cow is de horns on?

CORA

Embarrassed.

Aw, don't bring dat up. I'm sick of hearin' about dat farm.

ROCKY

You got nuttin' on us!

CORA

Ignoring this.

Me and dis overgrown tramp has been scrappin' about it. He says
Joisey's de best place, and I says Long Island because we'll be near
Coney. And I tells him, How do I know yuh're off of periodicals for
life? I don't give a damn how drunk yuh get, the way we are, but I
don't wanta be married to no soak.

CHUCK

And I tells her I'm off de stuff for life. Den she beefs we won't be
married a month before I'll trow it in her face she was a tart. "Jees,
Baby," I tells her. "Why should I? What de hell yuh tink I tink I'm
marryin', a voigin? Why should I kick as long as yuh lay off it and
don't do no cheatin' wid de iceman or nobody?

He gives her a rough hug.

Dat's on de level, Baby.

He kisses her.

CORA

Kissing him.

Aw, yuh big tramp!

ROCKY

Shakes his head with profound disgust.

Can yuh tie it? I'll buy a drink. I'll do anything.

He gets up.

CORA

No, dis round's on me. I run into luck. Dat's why I dragged Chuck outa bed to celebrate. It was a sailor. I rolled him.

She giggles.

Listen, it was a scream. I've run into some nutty souses, but dis guy was de nuttiest. De booze dey dish out around de Brooklyn Navy Yard must be as turrible bug-juice as Harry's. My dogs was givin' out when I seen dis guy holdin' up a lamppost, so I hurried to get him before a cop did. I says, "Hello, Handsome, wanta have a good time?" Jees, he was paralyzed! One of dem polite jags. He tries to bow to me, imagine, and I had to prop him up or he'd fell on his nose. And what d'yuh tink he said? "Lady," he says, "can yuh kindly tell me de nearest way to de Museum of Natural History?"

They all laugh.

Can yuh imagine! At two A.M. As if I'd know where de dump was anyway. But I says, "Sure ting, Honey Boy, I'll be only too glad." So I steered him into a side street where it was dark and propped him against a wall and give him a frisk.

She giggles.

And what d'yuh tink he does? Jees, I ain't lyin', he begins to laugh, de big sap! He says, "Quit ticklin' me." While I was friskin' him for his roll! I near died! Den I toined him 'round and give him a push to start him. "Just keep goin'," I told him. "It's a big white building on your right. You can't miss it." He must be swimmin' in de North River yet!

They all laugh.

CHUCK

Ain't Uncle Sam de sap to trust guys like dat wid dough!

CORA

With a business-like air.

I picked twelve bucks offa him. Come on, Rocky. Set 'em up.

ROCKY *goes back to the bar.* CORA *looks around the room.*

Say, Chuck's kiddin' about de iceman a minute ago reminds me. Where de hell's Hickey?

ROCKY

Dat's what we're all wonderin'.

CORA

He oughta be here. Me and Chuck seen him.

ROCKY

Excited, comes back from the bar, forgetting the drinks.
You seen Hickey?
He nudges HOPE.
Hey, Boss, come to! Cora's seen Hickey.
HOPE *is instantly wide awake and everyone in the place, except* HUGO
and PARRITT, *begins to rouse up hopefully, as if a mysterious wireless
message had gone round.*

HOPE

Where'd you see him, Cora?

CORA

Right on de next corner. He was standin' dere. We said, "Welcome
to our city. De gang is expectin' yuh wid deir tongues hangin' out
a yard long." And I kidded him, "How's de iceman, Hickey? How's
he doin' at your house?" He laughs and says, "Fine." And he says,
"Tell de gang I'll be along in a minute. I'm just finishin' figurin' out
de best way to save dem and bring dem peace."

HOPE

Chuckles.
Bejees, he's thought up a new gag! It's a wonder he didn't borry a
Salvation Army uniform and show up in that! Go out and get him,
Rocky. Tell him we're waitin' to be saved!
ROCKY *goes out, grinning.*

CORA

Yeah, Harry, he was only kiddin'. But he was funny, too, somehow.
He was different, or somethin'.

CHUCK

Sure, he was sober, Baby. Dat's what made him different. We ain't

never seen him when he wasn't on a drunk, or had de willies gettin'
over it.

CORA

Sure! Gee, ain't I dumb?

HOPE

With conviction.

The dumbest broad I ever seen!

Then puzzledly.

Sober? That's funny. He's always lapped up a good starter on his way
here. Well, bejees, he won't be sober long! He'll be good and ripe for
my birthday party tonight at twelve.

He chuckles with excited anticipation—addressing all of them.

Listen! He's fixed some new gag to pull on us. We'll pretend to let
him kid us, see? And we'll kid the pants off him.

*They all say laughingly, "Sure, Harry," "Righto," "That's the stuff,"
"We'll fix him," etc., etc., their faces excited with the same eager an-
ticipation.* ROCKY *appears in the doorway at the end of the bar with*
HICKEY, *his arm around* HICKEY'S *shoulders.*

ROCKY

With an affectionate grin.

Here's the old son of a bitch!

*They all stand up and greet him with affectionate acclaim, "Hello,
Hickey!" etc. Even* HUGO *comes out of his coma to raise his head and
blink through his thick spectacles with a welcoming giggle.*

HICKEY

Jovially.

Hello, Gang!

*He stands a moment, beaming around at all of them affectionately. He is
about fifty, a little under medium height, with a stout, roly-poly figure.
His face is round and smooth and big-boyish with bright blue eyes, a
button nose, a small, pursed mouth. His head is bald except for a fringe
of hair around his temples and the back of his head. His expression is
fixed in a salesman's winning smile of self-confident affability and hearty
good fellowship. His eyes have the twinkle of a humor which delights in
kidding others but can also enjoy equally a joke on himself. He exudes a*

friendly, generous personality that makes everyone like him on sight. You get the impression, too, that he must have real ability in his line. There is an efficient, business-like approach in his manner, and his eyes can take you in shrewdly at a glance. He has the salesman's mannerisms of speech, an easy flow of glib, persuasive convincingness. His clothes are those of a successful drummer whose territory consists of minor cities and small towns—not flashy but conspicuously spic and span. He immediately puts on an entrance act, places a hand affectedly on his chest, throws back his head, and sings in a falsetto tenor.

"It's always fair weather, when good fellows get together!"

Changing to a comic bass and another tune.

"And another little drink won't do us any harm!"

They all roar with laughter at this burlesque which his personality makes really funny. He waves his hand in a lordly manner to ROCKY.

Do your duty, Brother Rocky. Bring on the rat poison!

ROCKY *grins and goes behind the bar to get drinks amid an approving cheer from the crowd.* HICKEY *comes forward to shake hands with* HOPE—*with affectionate heartiness.*

How goes it, Governor?

HOPE

Enthusiastically.

Bejees, Hickey, you old bastard, it's good to see you!

HICKEY *shakes hands with* MOSHER *and* MCGLOIN; *leans right to shake hands with* MARGIE *and* PEARL; *moves to the middle table to shake hands with* LEWIS, JOE MOTT, WEJOEN *and* JIMMY; *waves to* WILLIE, LARRY *and* HUGO. *He greets each by name with the same affectionate heartiness and there is an interchange of "How's the kid?" "How's the old scout?" "How's the boy?" "How's everything?" etc., etc.* ROCKY *begins setting out drinks, whiskey glasses with chasers, and a bottle for each table, starting with* LARRY's *table.* HOPE *says.*

Sit down, Hickey. Sit down.

HICKY *takes the chair, facing front, at the front of the table in the second row which is half between* HOPE's *table and the one where* JIMMY TOMORROW *is.* HOPE *goes on with excited pleasure.*

Bejees, Hickey, it seems natural to see your ugly, grinning map.

With a scornful nod to CORA.

69

This dumb broad was tryin' to tell us you'd changed, but you ain't a damned bit. Tell us about yourself. How've you been doin'? Bejees, you look like a million dollars.

ROCKY

Coming to HICKEY's *table, puts a bottle of whiskey, a glass and a chaser on it—then hands* HICKEY *a key.*
Here's your key, Hickey. Same old room.

HICKEY

Shoves the key in his pocket.
Thanks, Rocky. I'm going up in a little while and grab a snooze. Haven't been able to sleep lately and I'm tired as hell. A couple of hours good kip will fix me.

HOPE

As ROCKY *puts drinks on his table.*
First time I ever heard you worry about sleep. Bejees, you never would go to bed.
He raises his glass, and all the others except PARRITT *do likewise.*
Get a few slugs under your belt and you'll forget sleeping. Here's mud in your eye, Hickey.
They all join in with the usual humorous toasts.

HICKEY

Heartily.
Drink hearty, boys and girls!
They all drink, but HICKEY *drinks only his chaser.*

HOPE

Bejees, is that a new stunt, drinking your chaser first?

HICKEY

No, I forgot to tell Rocky— You'll have to excuse me, boys and girls, but I'm off the stuff. For keeps.
They stare at him in amazed incredulity.

HOPE

What the hell—
Then with a wink at the others, kiddingly.

Sure! Joined the Salvation Army, ain't you? Been elected President of the W.C.T.U.? Take that bottle away from him, Rocky. We don't want to tempt him into sin.

He chuckles and the others laugh.

HICKEY

Earnestly.

No, honest, Harry. I know it's hard to believe but—

He pauses—then adds simply.

Cora was right, Harry. I have changed. I mean, about booze. I don't need it any more.

They all stare, hoping it's a gag, but impressed and disappointed and made vaguely uneasy by the change they now sense in him.

HOPE

His kidding a bit forced.

Yeah, go ahead, kid the pants off us! Bejees, Cora said you was coming to save us! Well, go on. Get this joke off your chest! Start the service! Sing a God-damned hymn if you like. We'll all join in the chorus. "No drunkard can enter this beautiful home." That's a good one.

He forces a cackle.

HICKEY

Grinning.

Oh, hell, Governor! You don't think I'd come around here peddling some brand of temperance bunk, do you? You know me better than that! Just because I'm through with the stuff don't mean I'm going Prohibition. Hell, I'm not that ungrateful! It's given me too many good times. I feel exactly the same as I always did. If anyone wants to get drunk, if that's the only way they can be happy, and feel at peace with themselves, why the hell shouldn't they? They have my full and entire sympathy. I know all about that game from soup to nuts. I'm the guy that wrote the book. The only reason I've quit is— Well, I finally had the guts to face myself and throw overboard the damned lying pipe dream that'd been making me miserable, and do what I had to do for the happiness of all concerned—and then all at once I found I was at peace with myself and I didn't need booze any more. That's all there was to it.

He pauses. They are starting at him, uneasy and beginning to feel defensive. HICKEY *looks round and grins affectionately—apologetically.*

But what the hell! Don't let me be a wet blanket, making fool speeches about myself. Set 'em up again, Rocky. Here.

He pulls a big roll from his pocket and peels off a ten-dollar bill. The faces of all brighten.

Keep the balls coming until this is killed. Then ask for more.

ROCKY

Jees, a roll dat'd choke a hippopotamus! Fill up, youse guys.

They all pour out drinks.

HOPE

That sounds more like you, Hickey. That water-wagon bull— Cut out the act and have a drink, for Christ's sake.

HICKEY

It's no act, Governor. But don't get me wrong. That don't mean I'm a teetotal grouch and can't be in the party. Hell, why d'you suppose I'm here except to have a party, same as I've always done, and help celebrate your birthday tonight? You've all been good pals to me, the best friends I've ever had. I've been thinking about you ever since I left the house—all the time I was walking over here—

HOPE

Walking? Bejees, do you mean to say you walked?

HICKEY

I sure did. All the way from the wilds of darkest Astoria. Didn't mind it a bit, either. I seemed to get here before I knew it. I'm a bit tired and sleepy but otherwise I feel great.

Kiddingly.

That ought to encourage you, Governor—show you a little walk around the ward is nothing to be so scared about.

He winks at the others. HOPE *stiffens resentfully for a second.* HICKEY *goes on.*

I didn't make such bad time either for a fat guy, considering it's a hell of a ways, and I sat in the park a while thinking. It was going on twelve when I went in the bedroom to tell Evelyn I was leaving. Six hours, say. No, less than that. I'd been standing on the corner some time before Cora and Chuck came along, thinking about all of you. Of course, I was only kidding Cora with that stuff about saving you. *Then seriously.*

No, I wasn't either. But I didn't mean booze. I meant save you from pipe dreams. I know now, from my experience, they're the things that really poison and ruin a guy's life and keep him from finding any peace. If you knew how free and contented I feel now. I'm like a new man. And the cure for them is so damned simple, once you have the nerve. Just the old dope of honesty is the best policy—honesty with yourself, I mean. Just stop lying about yourself and kidding yourself about tomorrows.

He is staring ahead of him now as if he were talking aloud to himself as much as to them. Their eyes are fixed on him with uneasy resentment. His manner becomes apologetic again.

Hell, this begins to sound like a damned sermon on the way to lead the good life. Forget that part of it. It's in my blood, I guess. My old man used to whale salvation into my heinie with a birch rod. He was a preacher in the sticks of Indiana, like I've told you. I got my knack of sales gab from him, too. He was the boy who could sell those Hoosier hayseeds building lots along the Golden Street! *Taking on a salesman's persuasiveness.*

Now listen, boys and girls, don't look at me as if I was trying to sell you a goldbrick. Nothing up my sleeve, honest. Let's take an example. Any one of you. Take you, Governor. That walk around the ward you never take—

HOPE
Defensively sharp.
What about it?

HICKEY
Grinning affectionately.
Why, you know as well as I do, Harry. Everything about it.

HOPE
Defiantly.
Bejees, I'm going to take it!

HICKEY
Sure, you're going to—this time. Because I'm going to help you. I know it's the thing you've got to do before you'll ever know what real peace means.
He looks at JIMMY TOMORROW.
Same thing with you, Jimmy. You've got to try and get your old job back. And no tomorrow about it!
As JIMMY *stiffens with a pathetic attempt at dignity—placatingly.*
No, don't tell me, Jimmy. I know all about tomorrow. I'm the guy that wrote the book.

JIMMY
I don't understand you. I admit I've foolishly delayed, but as it happens, I'd just made up my mind that as soon as I could get straightened out—

HICKEY
Fine! That's the spirit! And I'm going to help you. You've been damned kind to me, Jimmy, and I want to prove how grateful I am. When it's all over and you don't have to nag at yourself any more, you'll be grateful to me, too!
He looks around at the others.
And all the rest of you, ladies included, are in the same boat, one way or another.

LARRY
Who has been listening with sardonic appreciation—in his comically intense, crazy whisper.
Be God, you've hit the nail on the head, Hickey! This dump is the Palace of Pipe Dreams!

HICKEY
Grins at him with affectionate kidding.
Well, well! The Old Grandstand Foolosopher speaks! You think you're the big exception, eh? Life doesn't mean a damn to you any

more, does it? You're retired from the circus. You're just waiting impatiently for the end—the good old Long Sleep!

He chuckles.

Well, I think a lot of you, Larry, you old bastard. I'll try and make an honest man of you, too!

LARRY

Stung.

What the devil are you hinting at, anyway?

HICKEY

You don't have to ask me, do you, a wise old guy like you? Just ask yourself. I'll bet you know.

PARRITT

Is watching LARRY'S *face with a curious sneering satisfaction.*

He's got your number all right, Larry!

He turns to HICKEY.

That's the stuff, Hickey. Show the old faker up! He's got no right to sneak out of everything.

HICKEY

Regards him with surprise at first, then with a puzzled interest.

Hello. A stranger in our midst. I didn't notice you before, Brother.

PARRITT

Embarrassed, his eyes shifting away.

My name's Parritt. I'm an old friend of Larry's.

His eyes come back to HICKEY *to find him still sizing him up—defensively.*

Well? What are you staring at?

HICKEY

Continuing to stare—puzzledly.

No, offense, Brother. I was trying to figure— Haven't we met before some place?

PARRITT

Reassured.

No. First time I've ever been East.

HICKEY

No, you're right. I know that's not it. In my game, to be a shark at it, you teach yourself never to forget a name or a face. But still I know damned well I recognized something about you. We're members of the same lodge—in some way.

PARRITT

Uneasy again.

What are you talking about? You're nuts.

HICKEY

Dryly.

Don't try to kid me, Little Boy. I'm a good salesman—so damned good the firm was glad to take me back after every drunk—and what made me good was I could size up anyone.

Frowningly puzzled again.

But I don't see—

Suddenly breezily good-natured.

Never mind. I can tell you're having trouble with yourself and I'll be glad to do anything I can to help a friend of Larry's.

LARRY

Mind your own business, Hickey. He's nothing to you—or to me, either.

HICKEY *gives him a keen inquisitive glance.* LARRY *looks away and goes on sarcastically.*

You're keeping us all in suspense. Tell us more about how you're going to save us.

HICKEY

Good-naturedly but seeming a little hurt.

Hell, don't get sore, Larry. Not at me. We've always been good pals, haven't we? I know I've always liked you a lot.

LARRY

A bit shamefaced.

Well, so have I liked you. Forget it, Hickey.

HICKEY

Beaming.

76

Fine! That's the spirit!

Looking around at the others, who have forgotten their drinks.

What's the matter, everybody? What is this, a funeral? Come on and drink up! A little action!

They all drink.

Have another. Hell, this is a celebration! Forget it, if anything I've said sounds too serious. I don't want to be a pain in the neck. Any time you think I'm talking out of turn, just tell me to go chase myself!

He yawns with growing drowsiness and his voice grows a bit muffled.

No, boys and girls, I'm not trying to put anything over on you. It's just that I know now from experience what a lying pipe dream can do to you—and how damned relieved and contented with yourself you feel when you're rid of it.

He yawns again.

God, I'm sleepy all of a sudden. That long walk is beginning to get me. I better go upstairs. Hell of a trick to go dead on you like this.

He starts to get up but relaxes again. His eyes blink as he tries to keep them open.

No, boys and girls, I've never known what real peace was until now. It's a grand feeling, like when you're sick and suffering like hell and the Doc gives you a shot in the arm, and the pain goes, and you drift off.

His eyes close.

You can let go of yourself at last. Let yourself sink down to the bottom of the sea. Rest in peace. There's no farther you have to go. Not a single damned hope or dream left to nag you. You'll all know what I mean after you—

He pauses—mumbles.

Excuse—all in—got to grab forty winks— Drink up, everybody—on me—

The sleep of complete exhaustion overpowers him. His chin sags to his chest. They stare at him with puzzled uneasy fascination.

HOPE

Forcing a tone of irritation.

Bejees, that's a fine stunt, to go to sleep on us!

Then fumingly to the crowd.

Well, what the hell's the matter with you bums? Why don't you drink up? You're always crying for booze, and now you've got it under your nose, you sit like dummies!

They start and gulp down their whiskies and pour another. HOPE *stares at* HICKEY.

Bejees, I can't figure Hickey. I still say he's kidding us. Kid his own grandmother, Hickey would. What d'you think, Jimmy?

JIMMY
Unconvincingly.

It must be another of his jokes, Harry, although— Well, he does appear changed. But he'll probably be his natural self again tomorrow—

Hastily.

I mean, when he wakes up.

LARRY
Staring at HICKEY *frowningly—more aloud to himself than to them.*

You'll make a mistake if you think he's only kidding.

PARRITT
In a low confidential voice.

I don't like that guy, Larry. He's too damned nosy. I'm going to steer clear of him.

LARRY *gives him a suspicious glance, then looks hastily away.*

JIMMY
With an attempt at open-minded reasonableness.

Still, Harry, I have to admit there was some sense in his nonsense. It is time I got my job back—although I hardly need him to remind me.

HOPE
With an air of frankness.

Yes, and I ought to take a walk around the ward. But I don't need no Hickey to tell me, seeing I got it all set for my birthday tomorrow.

LARRY
Sardonically.

Ha!

Then in his comically intense, crazy whisper.

Be God, it looks like he's going to make two sales of his peace at least! But you'd better make sure first it's the real McCoy and not poison.

HOPE

Disturbed—angrily.

You bughouse I-Won't-Work harp, who asked you to shove in an oar? What the hell d'you mean, poison? Just because he has your number—

He immediately feels ashamed of this taunt and adds apologetically.

Bejees, Larry, you're always croaking about something to do with death. It gets my nanny. Come on, fellers, let's drink up.

They drink. HOPE's *eyes are fixed on* HICKEY *again.*

Stone cold sober and dead to the world! Spilling that business about pipe dreams! Bejees, I don't get it.

He bursts out again in angry complaint.

He ain't like the old Hickey! He'll be a fine wet blanket to have around at my birthday party! I wish to hell he'd never turned up!

MOSHER

Who has been the least impressed by HICKEY's *talk and is the first to recover and feel the effect of the drinks on top of his hangover—genially.*

Give him time, Harry, and he'll come out of it. I've watched many cases of almost fatal teetotalism, but they all came out of it completely cured and as drunk as ever. My opinion is the poor sap is temporarily bughouse from overwork.

Musingly.

You can't be too careful about work. It's the deadliest habit known to science, a great physician once told me. He practiced on street corners under a torchlight. He was positively the only doctor in the world who claimed that rattlesnake oil, rubbed on the prat, would cure heart failure in three days. I remember well his saying to me, "You are naturally delicate, Ed, but if you drink a pint of bad whiskey before breakfast every evening, and never work if you can help it, you may live to a ripe old age. It's staying sober and working that cuts men off in their prime."

While he is talking, they turn to him with eager grins. They are longing to laugh, and as he finishes they roar. Even PARRITT *laughs.* HICKEY *sleeps on like a dead man, but* HUGO, *who had passed into his customary coma again, head on table, looks up through his thick spectacles and giggles foolishly.*

HUGO
Blinking around at them. As the laughter dies he speaks in his giggling, wheedling manner, as if he were playfully teasing children.
Laugh, leedle bourgeois monkey-faces! Laugh like fools, leedle stupid peoples!
His tone suddenly changes to one of guttural soapbox denunciation and he pounds on the table with a small fist.
I vill laugh, too! But I vill laugh last! I vill laugh at you!
He declaims his favorite quotation.
"The days grow hot, O Babylon! 'Tis cool beneath thy villow trees!"
They all hoot him down in a chorus of amused jeering. HUGO *is not offended. This is evidently their customary reaction. He giggles goodnaturedly.* HICKEY *sleeps on. They have all forgotten their uneasiness about him now and ignore him.*

LEWIS
Tipsily.
Well, now that our little Robespierre has got the daily bit of guillotining off his chest, tell me more about your doctor friend, Ed. He strikes me as the only bloody sensible medico I ever heard of. I think we should appoint him house physician here without a moment's delay.
They all laughingly assent.

MOSHER
Warming to his subject, shakes his head sadly.
Too late! The old Doc has passed on to his Maker. A victim of overwork, too. He didn't follow his own advice. Kept his nose to the grindstone and sold one bottle of snake oil too many. Only eighty years old when he was taken. The saddest part was that he knew he was doomed. The last time we got paralyzed together he told me: "This game will get me yet, Ed. You see before you a broken

man, a martyr to medical science. If I had any nerves I'd have a nervous breakdown. You won't believe me, but this last year there was actually one night I had so many patients, I didn't even have time to get drunk. The shock to my system brought on a stroke which, as a doctor, I recognized was the beginning of the end." Poor old Doc! When he said this he started crying. "I hate to go before my task is completed, Ed," he sobbed. "I'd hoped I'd live to see the day when, thanks to my miraculous cure, there wouldn't be a single vacant cemetery lot left in this glorious country."

There is a roar of laughter. He waits for it to die and then goes on sadly.
I miss Doc. He was a gentleman of the old school. I'll bet he's standing on a street corner in hell right now, making suckers of the damned, telling them there's nothing like snake oil for a bad burn.

There is another roar of laughter. This time it penetrates HICKEY's *exhausted slumber. He stirs on his chair, trying to wake up, managing to raise his head a little and force his eyes half open. He speaks with a drowsy, affectionately encouraging smile. At once the laughter stops abruptly and they turn to him startledly.*

HICKEY
That's the spirit—don't let me be a wet blanket—all I want is to see you happy—
He slips back into heavy sleep again. They all stare at him, their faces again puzzled, resentful and uneasy.

CURTAIN

Act Two

The back room only. The black curtain dividing it from the bar is the right wall of the scene. It is getting on toward midnight of the same day.

The back room has been prepared for a festivity. At center, front, four of the circular tables are pushed together to form one long table with an uneven line of chairs behind it, and chairs at each end. This improvised banquet table is covered with old table cloths, borrowed from a neighboring beanery, and is laid with glasses, plates and cutlery before each of the seventeen chairs. Bottles of bar whiskey are placed at intervals within reach of any sitter. An old upright piano and stool have been moved in and stand against the wall at left, front. At right, front, is a table without chairs. The other tables and chairs that had been in the room have been moved out, leaving a clear floor space at rear for dancing. The floor has been swept clean of sawdust and scrubbed. Even the walls show evidence of having been washed, although the result is only to heighten their splotchy leprous look. The electric light brackets are adorned with festoons of red ribbon. In the middle of the separate table at right, front, is a birthday cake with six candles. Several packages, tied with ribbon, are also on the table. There are two necktie boxes, two cigar boxes, a fifth containing a half dozen handkerchiefs, the sixth is a square jeweler's watch box.

As the curtain rises, CORA, CHUCK, HUGO, LARRY, MARGIE, PEARL *and* ROCKY *are discovered.* CHUCK, ROCKY *and the three girls have dressed up for the occasion.* CORA *is arranging a bouquet of flowers in a vase, the vase being a big schooner glass from the bar, on top of the piano.* CHUCK *sits in a chair at the foot (left) of the banquet table. He has turned it so he can watch her. Near the middle of the row of chairs behind the table,* LARRY *sits, facing front, a drink of whiskey before him. He is staring before him in frowning, disturbed meditation. Next to him, on his left,* HUGO *is in his habitual position, passed out, arms on table, head on arms, a full whiskey glass by his head. By the separate table at right, front,* MARGIE *and* PEARL *are arranging the cake and presents, and* ROCKY *stands by them. All of them, with the exception of* CHUCK *and* ROCKY, *have had plenty to drink and show it, but no one, except* HUGO, *seems to be drunk. They are trying to act up in the spirit of the occasion but there is something forced about their manner, an undercurrent of nervous irritation and preoccupation.*

CORA
Standing back from the piano to regard the flower effect.
How's dat, Kid?

CHUCK
Grumpily.
What de hell do I know about flowers?

CORA
Yuh can see dey're pretty, can't yuh, yuh big dummy?

CHUCK
Mollifyingly.
Yeah, Baby, sure. If yuh like 'em, dey're aw right wid me.
CORA *goes back to give the schooner of flowers a few more touches.*

MARGIE
Admiring the cake.
Some cake, huh, Poil? Lookit! Six candles. Each for ten years.

PEARL
When do we light de candles, Rocky?

ROCKY
Grumpily.
Ask dat bughouse Hickey. He's elected himself boss of dis boith-day racket. Just before Harry comes down, he says. Den Harry blows dem out wid one breath, for luck. Hickey was goin' to have sixty

83

candles, but I says, Jees, if de old guy took dat big a breath, he'd croak himself.

MARGIE
Challengingly.
Well, anyways, it's some cake, ain't it?

ROCKY
Without enthusiasm.
Sure, it's aw right by me. But what de hell is Harry goin' to do wid a cake? If he ever et a hunk, it'd croak him.

PEARL
Jees, yuh're a dope! Ain't he, Margie?

MARGIE
A dope is right!

ROCKY
Stung.
You broads better watch your step or —

PEARL
Defiantly.
Or what?

MARGIE
Yeah! Or what?
They glare at him truculently.

ROCKY
Say, what de hell's got into youse? It'll be twelve o'clock and Harry's boithday before long. I ain't lookin' for no trouble.

PEARL
Ashamed.
Aw, we ain't neider, Rocky.
For the moment this argument subsides.

CORA
Over her shoulder to CHUCK — *acidly.*
A guy what can't see flowers is pretty must be some dumbbell.

CHUCK

Yeah? Well, if I was as dumb as you—
Then mollifyingly.
Jees, yuh got your scrappin' pants on, ain't yuh?
Grins goodnaturedly.
Hell, Baby, what's eatin' yuh? All I'm tinkin' is, flowers is dat louse Hickey's stunt. We never had no flowers for Harry's boithday before. What de hell can Harry do wid flowers? He don't know a cauliflower from a geranium.

ROCKY

Yeah, Chuck, it's like I'm tellin' dese broads about de cake. Dat's Hickey's wrinkle, too.
Bitterly.
Jees, ever since he woke up, yuh can't hold him. He's taken on de party like it was his boithday.

MARGIE

Well, he's payin' for everything, ain't he?

ROCKY

Aw, I don't mind de boithday stuff so much. What gets my goat is de way he's tryin' to run de whole dump and everyone in it. He's buttin' in all over de place, tellin' everybody where dey get off. On'y he don't really tell yuh. He just keeps hintin' around.

PEARL

Yeah. He was hintin' to me and Margie.

MARGIE

Yeah, de lousy drummer.

ROCKY

He just gives yuh an earful of dat line of bull about yuh got to be honest wid yourself and not kid yourself, and have de guts to be what yuh are. I got sore. I told him dat's aw right for de bums in dis dump. I hope he makes dem wake up. I'm sick of listenin' to dem hop dem-selves up. But it don't go wid me, see? I don't kid myself wid no pipe dream.

85

PEARL *and* MARGIE *exchange a derisive look. He catches it and his eyes narrow.*
What are yuh grinnin' at?

PEARL
Her face hard—scornfully.
Nuttin'.

MARGIE
Nuttin'.

ROCKY
It better be nuttin'! Don't let Hickey put no ideas in your nuts if you wanta stay healthy!
Then angrily.
I wish de louse never showed up! I hope he don't come back from de delicatessen. He's gettin' everyone nuts. He's ridin' someone every minute. He's got Harry and Jimmy Tomorrow run ragged, and de rest is hidin' in deir rooms so dey won't have to listen to him. Dey're all actin' cagey wid de booze, too, like dey was scared if dey get too drunk, dey might spill deir guts, or somethin'. And everybody's gettin' a prize grouch on.

CORA
Yeah, he's been hintin' round to me and Chuck, too. Yuh'd tink he suspected me and Chuck hadn't no real intention of gettin' married. Yuh'd tink he suspected Chuck wasn't goin' to lay off periodicals—or maybe even didn't want to.

CHUCK
He didn't say it right out or I'da socked him one. I told him, "I'm on de wagon for keeps and Cora knows it."

CORA
I told him, "Sure, I know it. And Chuck ain't never goin' to trow it in my face dat I was a tart, neider. And if yuh think we're just kiddin' ourselves, we'll show yuh!"

CHUCK
We're goin' to show him!

CORA

We got it all fixed. We've decided Joisey is where we want de farm, and we'll get married dere, too, because yuh don't need no license. We're goin' to get married tomorrow. Ain't we, Honey?

CHUCK

You bet, Baby.

ROCKY

Disgusted.

Christ, Chuck, are yuh lettin' dat bughouse louse Hickey kid yuh into—

CORA

Turns on him angrily.

Nobody's kiddin' him into it, nor me neider! And Hickey's right. If dis big tramp's goin' to marry me, he ought to do it, and not just shoot off his old bazoo about it.

ROCKY

Ignoring her.

Yuh can't be dat dumb, Chuck.

CORA

You keep outa dis! And don't start beefin' about crickets on de farm drivin' us nuts. You and your crickets! Yuh'd tink dey was elephants!

MARGIE

Coming to ROCKY's *defense—sneeringly.*

Don't notice dat broad, Rocky. Yuh heard her say "tomorrow," didn't yuh? It's de same old crap.

CORA

Glares at her.

Is dat so?

PEARL

Lines up with MARGIE—*sneeringly.*

Imagine Cora a bride! Dat's a hot one! Jees, Cora, if all de guys you've stayed wid was side by side, yuh could walk on 'em from here to Texas!

CORA
Starts moving toward her threateningly.
Yuh can't talk like dat to me, yuh fat Dago hooker! I may be a tart, but I ain't a cheap old whore like you!

PEARL
Furiously.
I'll show yuh who's a whore!
They start to fly at each other, but CHUCK *and* ROCKY *grab them from behind.*

CHUCK
Forcing CORA *onto a chair.*
Sit down and cool off, Baby.

ROCKY
Doing the same to PEARL.
Nix on de rough stuff, Poil.

MARGIE
Glaring at CORA.
Why don't you leave Poil alone, Rocky? She'll fix dat blonde's clock! Or if she don't, I will!

ROCKY
Shut up, you!
Disgustedly.
Jees, what dames! D'yuh wanta gum Harry's party?

PEARL
A bit shamefaced—sulkily.
Who wants to? But nobody can't call me a —.

ROCKY
Exasperatedly.
Aw, bury it! What are you, a voigin?
PEARL *stares at him, her face growing hard and bitter. So does* MARGIE.

PEARL

Yuh mean you tink I'm a whore, too, huh?

MARGIE

Yeah, and me?

ROCKY

Now don't start nuttin'!

PEARL

I suppose it'd tickle you if me and Margie did what dat louse, Hickey, was hintin' and came right out and admitted we was whores.

ROCKY

Aw right! What of it? It's de truth, ain't it?

CORA

Lining up with PEARL *and* MARGIE—*indignantly.*
Jees, Rocky, dat's a fine hell of a ting to say to two goils dat's been as good to yuh as Poil and Margie!
To PEARL.
I didn't mean to call yuh dat, Poil. I was on'y mad.

PEARL

Accepts the apology gratefully.
Sure, I was mad, too, Cora. No hard feelin's.

ROCKY

Relieved.
Dere. Dat fixes everyting, don't it?

PEARL

Turns on him—hard and bitter.
Aw right, Rocky. We're whores. You know what dat makes you, don't you?

ROCKY

Angrily.
Look out, now!

MARGIE

A lousy little pimp, dat's what!

ROCKY

I'll loin yuh!

He gives her a slap on the side of the face.

PEARL

A dirty little Ginny pimp, dat's what!

ROCKY

Gives her a slap, too.

And dat'll loin you!

But they only stare at him with hard sneering eyes.

MARGIE

He's provin' it to us, Poil.

PEARL

Yeah! Hickey's convoited him. He's give up his pipe dream!

ROCKY

Furious and at the same time bewildered by their defiance.

Lay off me or I'll beat de hell—

CHUCK

Growls.

Aw, lay off dem. Harry's party ain't no time to beat up your stable.

ROCKY

Turns to him.

Whose stable? Who d'yuh tink yuh're talkin' to? I ain't never beat dem up! What d'yuh tink I am? I just give dem a slap, like any guy would his wife, if she got too gabby. Why don't yuh tell dem to lay off me? I don't want no trouble on Harry's boithday party.

MARGIE

A victorious gleam in her eye—tauntingly.

Aw right, den, yuh poor little Ginny. I'll lay off yuh till de party's over if Poil will.

PEARL

Tauntingly.

Sure, I will. For Harry's sake, not yours, yuh little Wop!

ROCKY

Stung.

Say, listen, youse! Don't get no wrong idea—

But an interruption comes from LARRY *who bursts into a sardonic laugh. They all jump startledly and look at him with unanimous hostility.* ROCKY *transfers his anger to him.*

Who de hell yuh laughin' at, yuh half-dead old stew bum?

CORA

Sneeringly.

At himself, he ought to be! Jees, Hickey's sure got his number!

LARRY

Ignoring them, turns to HUGO *and shakes him by the shoulder—in his comically intense, crazy whisper.*

Wake up, Comrade! Here's the Revolution starting on all sides of you and you're sleeping through it! Be God, it's not to Bakunin's ghost you ought to pray in your dreams, but to the great Nihilist, Hickey! He's started a movement that'll blow up the world!

HUGO

Blinks at him through his thick spectacles—with guttural denunciation.

You, Larry! Renegade! Traitor! I vill have you shot!

He giggles.

Don't be a fool! Buy me a trink!

He sees the drink in front of him, and gulps it down. He begins to sing the Carmagnole in a guttural basso, pounding on the table with his glass.

"Dansons la Carmagnole! Vive le son! Vive le son! Dansons la Carmagnole! Vive le son des canons!"

ROCKY

Can dat noise!

HUGO

Ignores this—to LARRY, *in a low tone of hatred.*

That bourgeois svine, Hickey! He laughs like good fellow, he makes jokes, he dares make hints to me so I see what he dares to think. He thinks I am finish, it is too late, and so I do not vish the Day come because it vill not be my Day. Oh, I see what he thinks! He thinks lies even vorse, dat I—

He stops abruptly with a guilty look, as if afraid he was letting something slip—then revengefully.

I vill have him hanged the first one of all on de first lamppost!

He changes his mood abruptly and peers around at ROCKY *and the others—giggling again.*

Vhy you so serious, leedle monkey-faces? It's all great joke, no? So ve get drunk, and ve laugh like hell, and den ve die, and de pipe dream vanish!

A bitter mocking contempt creeps into his tone.

But be of good cheer, leedle stupid peoples! "The days grow hot, O Babylon!" Soon, leedle proletarians, ve vill have free picnic in the cool shade, ve vill eat hot dogs and trink free beer beneath the villow trees! Like hogs, yes! Like beautiful leedle hogs!

He stops startledly, as if confused and amazed at what he has heard himself say. He mutters with hatred.

Dot Gottamned liar, Hickey. It is he who makes me sneer. I want to sleep.

He lets his head fall forward on his folded arms again and closes his eyes. LARRY *gives him a pitying look, then quickly drinks his drink.*

CORA
Uneasily.
Hickey ain't overlookin' no bets, is he? He's even give Hugo de woiks.

LARRY
I warned you this morning he wasn't kidding.

MARGIE
Sneering.
De old wise guy!

PEARL
Yeah, still pretendin' he's de one exception, like Hickey told him. He don't do no pipe dreamin'! Oh, no!

LARRY
Sharply resentful.
I—!

Then abruptly he is drunkenly good-natured, and you feel this drunken manner is an evasive exaggeration.

All right, take it out on me, if it makes you more content. Sure, I love every hair of your heads, my great big beautiful baby dolls, and there's nothing I wouldn't do for you!

PEARL

Stiffly.

De old Irish bunk, huh? We ain't big. And we ain't your baby dolls! *Suddenly she is mollified and smiles.*

But we admit we're beautiful. Huh, Margie?

MARGIE

Smiling.

Sure ting! But what would he do wid beautiful dolls, even if he had de price, de old goat? *She laughs teasingly—then pats* LARRY *on the shoulder affectionately.*

Aw, yuh're aw right at dat, Larry, if yuh are full of bull!

PEARL

Sure. Yuh're aces wid us. We're noivous, dat's all. Dat lousy drummer —why can't he be like he's always been? I never seen a guy change so. You pretend to be such a fox, Larry. What d'yuh tink's happened to him?

LARRY

I don't know. With all his gab I notice he's kept that to himself so far. Maybe he's saving the great revelation for Harry's party. *Then irritably.*

To hell with him! I don't want to know. Let him mind his own business and I'll mind mine.

CHUCK

Yeah, dat's what I say.

CORA

Say, Larry, where's dat young friend of yours disappeared to?

LARRY

I don't care where he is, except I wish it was a thousand miles away!

Then, as he sees they are surprised at his vehemence, he adds hastily.
He's a pest.

ROCKY
Breaks in with his own preoccupation.
I don't give a damn what happened to Hickey, but I know what's gonna happen if he don't watch his step. I told him, "I'll take a lot from you, Hickey, like everyone else in dis dump, because yuh've always been a grand guy. But dere's tings I don't take from you nor nobody, see? Remember dat, or you'll wake up in a hospital—or maybe worse, wid your wife and de iceman walkin' slow behind yuh."

CORA
Aw, yuh shouldn't make dat iceman crack, Rocky. It's aw right for him to kid about it but—I notice Hickey ain't pulled dat old iceman gag dis time.
Excitedly.
D'yuh suppose dat he did catch his wife cheatin'? I don't mean wid no iceman, but wid some guy.

ROCKY
Aw, dat's de bunk. He ain't pulled dat gag or showed her photo around because he ain't drunk. And if he'd caught her cheatin' he'd be drunk, wouldn't he? He'd have beat her up and den gone on de woist drunk he'd ever staged. Like any other guy'd do.
The girls nod, convinced by this reasoning.

CHUCK
Sure! Rocky's got de right dope, Baby. He'd be paralyzed.
While he is speaking, the Negro, JOE, *comes in from the hallway. There is a noticeable change in him. He walks with a tough, truculent swagger and his good-natured face is set in sullen suspicion.*

JOE
To ROCKY—*defiantly.*
I's stood tellin' people dis dump is closed for de night all I's goin' to. Let Harry hire a doorman, pay him wages, if he wants one.

ROCKY
Scowling.
Yeah? Harry's pretty damned good to you.

JOE
Shamefaced.
Sure he is. I don't mean dat. Anyways, it's all right. I told Schwartz,
de cop, we's closed for de party. He'll keep folks away.
Aggressively again.
I want a big drink, dat's what!

CHUCK
Who's stoppin' yuh? Yuh can have all yuh want on Hickey.

JOE
Has taken a glass from the table and has his hand on a bottle when
HICKEY's *name is mentioned. He draws his hand back as if he were
going to refuse—then grabs it defiantly and pours a big drink.*
All right, I's earned all de drinks on him I could drink in a year for
listenin' to his crazy bull. And here's hopin' he gets de lockjaw!
He drinks and pours out another.
I drinks on him but I don't drink wid him. No, suh, never no more!

ROCKY
Aw, bull! Hickey's aw right. What's he done to you?

JOE
Sullenly.
Dat's my business. I ain't buttin' in yours, is I?
Bitterly.
Sure, you think he's all right. He's a white man, ain't he?
His tone becomes aggressive.
Listen to me, you white boys! Don't you get it in your heads I's pre-
tendin' to be what I ain't, or dat I ain't proud to be what I is, get me?
Or you and me's goin' to have trouble!
*He picks up his drink and walks left as far away from them as he can get
and slumps down on the piano stool.*

MARGIE
In a low angry tone.

What a noive! Just because we act nice to him, he gets a swelled nut! If dat ain't a coon all over!

CHUCK

Talkin' fight talk, huh? I'll moider de nigger!

He takes a threatening step toward JOE, *who is staring before him guiltily now.*

JOE

Speaks up shamefacedly.

Listen, boys, I's sorry. I didn't mean dat. You been good friends to me. I's nuts, I guess. Dat Hickey, he gets my head all mixed up wit craziness.

Their faces at once clear of resentment against him.

CORA

Aw, dat's aw right, Joe. De boys wasn't takin' yuh serious.

Then to the others, forcing a laugh.

Jees, what'd I say, Hickey ain't overlookin' no bets. Even Joe.

She pauses—then adds puzzledly.

De funny ting is, yuh can't stay sore at de bum when he's around. When he forgets de bughouse preachin', and quits tellin' yuh where yuh get off, he's de same old Hickey. Yuh can't help likin' de louse. And yuh got to admit he's got de right dope—

She adds hastily.

I mean, on some of de bums here.

MARGIE

With a sneering look at ROCKY.

Yeah, he's coitinly got one guy I know sized up right! Huh, Poil?

PEARL

He coitinly has!

ROCKY

Cut it out, I told yuh!

LARRY

Is staring before him broodingly. He speaks more aloud to himself than to them.

96

It's nothing to me what happened to him. But I have a feeling he's dying to tell us, inside him, and yet he's afraid. He's like that damned kid. It's strange the queer way he seemed to recognize him. If he's afraid, it explains why he's off booze. Like that damned kid again. Afraid if he got drunk, he'd tell—

While he is speaking, HICKEY *comes in the doorway at rear. He looks the same as in the previous act, except that now his face beams with the excited expectation of a boy going to a party. His arms are piled with packages.*

HICKEY

Booms in imitation of a familiar Polo Grounds bleacherite cry—with rising volume.

Well! Well!! Well!!!

They all jump startledly. He comes forward, grinning.

Here I am in the nick of time. Give me a hand with these bundles, somebody.

MARGIE *and* PEARL *start taking them from his arms and putting them on the table. Now that he is present, all their attitudes show the reaction* CORA *has expressed. They can't help liking him and forgiving him.*

MARGIE

Jees, Hickey, yuh scared me outa a year's growth, sneakin' in like dat.

HICKEY

Sneaking? Why, me and the taxi man made enough noise getting my big surprise in the hall to wake the dead. You were all so busy drinking in words of wisdom from the Old Wise Guy here, you couldn't hear anything else.

He grins at LARRY.

From what I heard, Larry, you're not so good when you start playing Sherlock Holmes. You've got me all wrong. I'm not afraid of anything now—not even myself. You better stick to the part of Old Cemetery, the Barker for the Big Sleep—that is, if you can still let yourself get away with it!

He chuckles and gives LARRY *a friendly slap on the back.* LARRY *gives him a bitter angry look.*

CORA

Giggles.

Old Cemetery! That's him, Hickey. We'll have to call him dat.

HICKEY

Watching LARRY *quizzically.*

Beginning to do a lot of puzzling about me, aren't you, Larry? But
that won't help you. You've got to think of yourself. I couldn't give
you my peace. You've got to find your own. All I can do is help you,
and the rest of the gang, by showing you the way to find it.

*He has said this with a simple persuasive earnestness. He pauses, and for
a second they stare at him with fascinated resentful uneasiness.*

ROCKY

Breaks the spell.

Aw, hire a church!

HICKEY

Placatingly.

All right! All right! Don't get sore, boys and girls. I guess that did
sound too much like a lousy preacher. Let's forget it and get busy on
the party.

They look relieved.

CHUCK

Is dose bundles grub, Hickey? You bought enough already to feed
an army.

HICKEY

With boyish excitement again.

Can't be too much! I want this to be the biggest birthday Harry's
ever had. You and Rocky go in the hall and get the big surprise. My
arms are busted lugging it.

They catch his excitement. CHUCK *and* ROCKY *go out, grinning expec-
tantly. The three girls gather around* HICKEY, *full of thrilled curiosity.*

PEARL

Jees, yuh got us all het up! What is it, Hickey?

HICKEY

Wait and see. I got it as a treat for the three of you more than anyone. I thought to myself, I'll bet this is what will please those whores
more than anything.

*They wince as if he had slapped them, but before they have a chance to
be angry, he goes on affectionately.*

I said to myself, I don't care how much it costs, they're worth it.
They're the best little scouts in the world, and they've been damned
kind to me when I was down and out! Nothing is too good for them.

Earnestly.

I mean every word of that, too—and then some!

Then, as if he noticed the expression on their faces for the first time.

What's the matter? You look sore. What—?

Then he chuckles.

Oh, I see. But you know how I feel about that. You know I didn't
say it to offend you. So don't be silly now.

MARGIE

Lets out a tense breath.

Aw right, Hickey. Let it slide.

HICKEY

Jubilantly, as CHUCK *and* ROCKY *enter carrying a big wicker basket.*

Look! There it comes! Unveil it, boys.

*They pull off a covering burlap bag. The basket is piled with quarts of
champagne.*

PEARL

With childish excitement.

It's champagne! Jees, Hickey, if you ain't a sport!

She gives him a hug, forgetting all animosity, as do the other girls.

MARGIE

I never been soused on champagne. Let's get stinko, Poil.

PEARL

You betcha my life! De bot' of us!

A holiday spirit of gay festivity has seized them all. Even JOE MOTT

is standing up to look at the wine with an admiring grin, and HUGO
raises his head to blink at it.

JOE

You sure is hittin' de high spots, Hickey.
Boastfully.
Man, when I runs my gambling' house, I drinks dat old bubbly water
in steins!
He stops guiltily and gives HICKEY *a look of defiance.*
I's goin' to drink it dat way again, too, soon's I make my stake! And
dat ain't no pipe dream, neider!
He sits down where he was, his back turned to them.

ROCKY

What'll we drink it outa, Hickey? Dere ain't no wine glasses.

HICKEY

Enthusiastically.
Joe has the right idea! Schooners! That's the spirit for Harry's birthday!
ROCKY *and* CHUCK *carry the basket of wine into the bar. The three
girls go back and stand around the entrance to the bar, chatting excited
among themselves and to* CHUCK *and* ROCKY *in the bar.*

HUGO

With his silly giggle.
Ve vill trink vine beneath the villow trees!

HICKEY

Grins at him.
That's the spirit, Brother—and let the lousy slaves drink vinegar!
HUGO *blinks at him startledly, then looks away.*

HUGO

Mutters.
Gottamned liar!
*He puts his head back on his arms and closes his eyes, but this time his
habitual pass-out has a quality of hiding.*

LARRY

Gives HUGO *a pitying glance—in a low tone of anger.*

Leave Hugo be! He rotted ten years in prison for his faith! He's earned his dream! Have you no decency or pity?

HICKEY

Quizzically.

Hello, what's this? I thought you were in the grandstand.

Then with a simple earnestness, taking a chair by LARRY, *and putting a hand on his shoulder.*

Listen, Larry, you're getting me all wrong. Hell, you ought to know me better. I've always been the best-natured slob in the world. Of course, I have pity. But now I've seen the light, it isn't my old kind of pity—the kind yours is. It isn't the kind that lets itself off easy by encouraging some poor guy to go on kidding himself with a lie—the kind that leaves the poor slob worse off because it makes him feel guiltier than ever—the kind that makes his lying hopes nag at him and reproach him until he's a rotten skunk in his own eyes. I know all about that kind of pity. I've had a bellyful of it in my time, and it's all wrong!

With a salesman's persuasiveness.

No, sir. The kind of pity I feel now is after final results that will really save the poor guy, and make him contented with what he is, and quit battling himself, and find peace for the rest of his life. Oh, I know how you resent the way I have to show you up to yourself. I don't blame you. I know from my own experience it's bitter medicine, facing yourself in the mirror with the old false whiskers off. But you forget that, once you're cured. You'll be grateful to me when all at once you find you're able to admit, without feeling ashamed, that all the grandstand foolosopher bunk and the waiting for the Big Sleep stuff is a pipe dream. You'll say to yourself, I'm just an old man who is scared of life, but even more scared of dying. So I'm keeping drunk and hanging on to life at any price, and what of it? Then you'll know what real peace means, Larry, because you won't be scared of either life or death any more. You simply won't give a damn! Any more than I do!

LARRY

Has been staring into his eyes with a fascinated wondering dread.
Be God, if I'm not beginning to think you've gone mad!
With a rush of anger.
You're a liar!

HICKEY

Injuredly.
Now, listen, that's no way to talk to an old pal who's trying to help
you. Hell, if you really wanted to die, you'd just take a hop off your
fire escape, wouldn't you? And if you really were in the grandstand,
you wouldn't be pitying everyone. Oh, I know the truth is tough at
first. It was for me. All I ask is for you to suspend judgment and give
it a chance. I'll absolutely guarantee— Hell, Larry, I'm no fool. Do
you suppose I'd deliberately set out to get under everyone's skin and
put myself in dutch with all my old pals, if I wasn't certain, from
my own experience, that it means contentment in the end for all of
you?
LARRY *again is staring at him fascinatedly.* HICKEY *grins.*
As for my being bughouse, you can't crawl out of it that way. Hell,
I'm too damned sane. I can size up guys, and turn 'em inside out,
better than I ever could. Even where they're strangers like that Parritt
kid. He's licked, Larry. I think there is only one possible way out you
can help him to take. That is, if you have the right kind of pity for
him.

LARRY

Uneasily.
What do you mean?
Attempting indifference.
I'm not advising him, except to leave me out of his troubles. He's
nothing to me.

HICKEY

Shakes his head.
You'll find he won't agree to that. He'll keep after you until he makes
you help him. Because he has to be punished, so he can forgive him-

self. He's lost all his guts. He can't manage it alone, and you're the only one he can turn to.

LARRY

For the love of God, mind your own business!
With forced scorn.
A lot you know about him! He's hardly spoken to you!

HICKEY

No, that's right. But I do know a lot about him just the same. I've had hell inside me. I can spot it in others.
Frowning.
Maybe that's what gives me the feeling there's something familiar about him, something between us.
He shakes his head.
No, it's more than that. I can't figure it. Tell me about him. For instance, I don't imagine he's married, is he?

LARRY

No.

HICKEY

Hasn't he been mixed up with some woman? I don't mean trollops. I mean the old real love stuff that crucifies you.

LARRY

With a calculating relieved look at him—encouraging him along this line.
Maybe you're right. I wouldn't be surprised.

HICKEY

Grins at him quizzically.
I see. You think I'm on the wrong track and you're glad I am. Because then I won't suspect whatever he did about the Great Cause. That's another lie you tell yourself, Larry, that the good old Cause means nothing to you any more.
LARRY *is about to burst out in denial but* HICKEY *goes on.*
But you're all wrong about Parritt. That isn't what's got him stopped. It's what's behind that. And it's a woman. I recognize the symptoms.

LARRY

Sneeringly.

And you're the boy who's never wrong! Don't be a damned fool. His trouble is he was brought up a devout believer in the Movement and now he's lost his faith. It's a shock, but he's young and he'll soon find another dream just as good.

He adds sardonically.

Or as bad.

HICKEY

All right. I'll let it go at that, Larry. He's nothing to me except I'm glad he's here because he'll help me make you wake up to yourself. I don't even like the guy, or the feeling there's anything between us. But you'll find I'm right just the same, when you get to the final showdown with him.

LARRY

There'll be no showdown! I don't give a tinker's damn—

HICKEY

Sticking to the old grandstand, eh? Well, I knew you'd be the toughest to convince of all the gang, Larry. And, along with Harry and Jimmy Tomorrow, you're the one I want most to help.

He puts an arm around LARRY'*s shoulder and gives him an affectionate hug.*

I've always liked you a lot, you old bastard!

He gets up and his manner changes to his bustling party excitement— glancing at his watch.

Well, well, not much time before twelve. Let's get busy, boys and girls.

He looks over the table where the cake is.

Cake all set. Good. And my presents, and yours, girls, and Chuck's, and Rocky's. Fine. Harry'll certainly be touched by your thought of him.

He goes back to the girls.

You go in the bar, Pearl and Margie, and get the grub ready so it can be brought right in. There'll be some drinking and toasts first, of course. My idea is to use the wine for that, so get it all set. I'll go upstairs now and root everyone out. Harry the last. I'll come back with him. Somebody light the candles on the cake when you hear us coming, and you start playing Harry's favorite tune, Cora. Hustle now, everybody. We want this to come off in style.

He bustles into the hall. MARGIE *and* PEARL *disappear in the bar.* CORA *goes to the piano.* JOE *gets off the stool sullenly to let her sit down.*

CORA

I got to practice. I ain't laid my mits on a box in Gawd knows when. *With the soft pedal down, she begins gropingly to pick out "The Sunshine of Paradise Alley."*
Is dat right, Joe? I've forgotten dat has-been tune.
She picks out a few more notes.
Come on, Joe, hum de tune so I can follow.
JOE *begins to hum and sing in a low voice and correct her. He forgets his sullenness and becomes his old self again.*

LARRY

Suddenly gives a laugh—in his comically intense, crazy tone.
Be God, it's a second feast of Belshazzar, with Hickey to do the writing on the wall!

CORA

Aw, shut up, Old Cemetery! Always beefin'!
WILLIE *comes in from the hall. He is in a pitiable state, his face pasty, haggard with sleeplessness and nerves, his eyes sick and haunted. He is sober.* CORA *greets him over her shoulder kiddingly.*
If it ain't Prince Willie!
Then kindly.
Gee, kid, yuh look sick. Get a coupla shots in yuh.

WILLIE

Tensely.
No, thanks. Not now. I'm tapering off.
He sits down weakly on LARRY's *right.*

CORA

Astonished.
What d'yuh know? He means it!

WILLIE

Leaning toward LARRY *confidentially—in a low shaken voice.*

It's been hell up in that damned room, Larry! The things I've imagined!

He shudders.

I thought I'd go crazy.

With pathetic boastful pride.

But I've got it beat now. By tomorrow morning I'll be on the wagon. I'll get back my clothes the first thing. Hickey's loaning me the money. I'm going to do what I've always said—go to the D.A.'s office. He was a good friend of my Old Man's. He was only assistant, then. He was in on the graft, but my Old Man never squealed on him. So he certainly owes it to me to give me a chance. And he knows that I really was a brilliant law student.

Self-reassuringly.

Oh, I know I can make good, now I'm getting off the booze forever.

Moved.

I owe a lot to Hickey. He's made me wake up to myself—see what a fool— It wasn't nice to face but—

With bitter resentment.

It isn't what he says. It's what you feel behind—what he hints— Christ, you'd think all I really wanted to do with my life was sit here and stay drunk.

With hatred.

I'll show him!

LARRY

Masking pity behind a sardonic tone.

If you want my advice, you'll put the nearest bottle to your mouth until you don't give a damn for Hickey!

WILLIE

Stares at a bottle greedily, tempted for a moment—then bitterly.

That's fine advice! I thought you were my friend!

He gets up with a hurt glance at LARRY, *and moves away to take a chair in back of the left end of the table, where he sits in dejected, shaking misery, his chin on his chest.*

JOE

To CORA.

No, like dis.

He beats time with his finger and sings in a low voice.

"She is the sunshine of Paradise Alley."

She plays.

Dat's more like it. Try it again.

She begins to play through the chorus again. DON PARRITT *enters from the hall. There is a frightened look on his face. He slinks in furtively, as if he were escaping from someone. He looks relieved when he sees* LARRY *and comes and slips into the chair on his right.* LARRY *pretends not to notice his coming, but he instinctively shrinks with repulsion.* PARRITT *leans toward him and speaks ingratiatingly in a low secretive tone.*

PARRITT

Gee, I'm glad you're here, Larry. That damned fool, Hickey, knocked on my door. I opened up because I thought it must be you, and he came busting in and made me come downstairs. I don't know what for. I don't belong in this birthday celebration. I don't know this gang and I don't want to be mixed up with them. All I came here for was to find you.

LARRY

Tensely.

I've warned you—

PARRITT

Goes on as if he hadn't heard.

Can't you make Hickey mind his own business? I don't like that guy, Larry. The way he acts, you'd think he had something on me. Why, just now he pats me on the shoulder, like he was sympathizing with me, and says, "I know how it is, Son, but you can't hide from yourself, not even here on the bottom of the sea. You've got to face the truth and then do what must be done for your own peace and the happiness of all concerned." What did he mean by that, Larry?

LARRY

How the hell would I know?

PARRITT

Then he grins and says, "Never mind, Larry's getting wise to him-self. I think you can rely on his help in the end. He'll have to choose between living and dying, and he'll never choose to die while there is a breath left in the old bastard!" And then he laughs like it was a joke on you.

He pauses. LARRY *is rigid on his chair, staring before him.* PARRITT *asks him with a sudden taunt in his voice.*

Well, what do you say to that, Larry?

LARRY

I've nothing to say. Except you're a bigger fool than he is to listen to him.

PARRITT

With a sneer.

Is that so? He's no fool where you're concerned. He's got your num-ber, all right!

LARRY'S *face tightens but he keeps silent.* PARRITT *changes to a contrite, appealing air.*

I don't mean that. But you keep acting as if you were sore at me, and that gets my goat. You know what I want most is to be friends with you, Larry. I haven't a single friend left in the world. I hoped you—

Bitterly.

And you could be, too, without it hurting you. You ought to, for Mother's sake. She really loved you. You loved her, too, didn't you?

LARRY

Tensely.

Leave what's dead in its grave.

PARRITT

I suppose, because I was only a kid, you didn't think I was wise about you and her. Well, I was. I've been wise, ever since I can remember, to all the guys she's had, although she'd tried to kid me along it wasn't so. That was a silly stunt for a free Anarchist woman, wasn't it, being ashamed of being free?

LARRY

Shut your damned trap!

PARRITT

Guiltily but with a strange undertone of satisfaction.

Yes, I know I shouldn't say that now. I keep forgetting she isn't free any more.

He pauses.

Do you know, Larry, you're the one of them all she cared most about? Anyone else who left the Movement would have been dead to her, but she couldn't forget you. She'd always make excuses for you. I used to try and get her goat about you. I'd say, "Larry's got brains and yet he thinks the Movement is just a crazy pipe dream." She'd blame it on booze getting you. She'd kid herself that you'd give up booze and come back to the Movement—tomorrow! She'd say, "Larry can't kill in himself a faith he's given his life to, not without killing himself."

He grins sneeringly.

How about it, Larry? Was she right?

LARRY *remains silent. He goes on insistently.*

I suppose what she really meant was, come back to her. She was always getting the Movement mixed up with herself. But I'm sure she really must have loved you, Larry. As much as she could love anyone besides herself. But she wasn't faithful to you, even at that, was she? That's why you finally walked out on her, isn't it? I remember that last fight you had with her. I was listening. I was on your side, even if she was my mother, because I liked you so much; you'd been so good to me—like a father. I remember her putting on her high-and-mighty free-woman stuff, saying you were still a slave to bourgeois morality and jealousy and you thought a woman you loved was a piece of private property you owned. I remember that you got mad and you told her, "I don't like living with a whore, if that's what you mean!"

LARRY

Bursts out.

You lie! I never called her that!

PARRITT

Goes on as if LARRY *hadn't spoken.*

I think that's why she still respects you, because it was you who left her. You were the only one to beat her to it. She got sick of the others before they did of her. I don't think she ever cared much about them, anyway. She just had to keep on having lovers to prove to herself how free she was.

He pauses—then with a bitter repulsion.

It made home a lousy place. I felt like you did about it. I'd get feeling it was like living in a whorehouse—only worse, because she didn't have to make her living—

LARRY

You bastard! She's your mother! Have you no shame?

PARRITT

Bitterly.

No! She brought me up to believe that family-respect stuff is all bourgeois, property-owning crap. Why should I be ashamed?

LARRY

Making a move to get up.

I've had enough!

PARRITT

Catches his arm—pleadingly.

No! Don't leave me! Please! I promise I won't mention her again!

LARRY *sinks back in his chair.*

I only did it to make you understand better. I know this isn't the place to— Why didn't you come up to my room, like I asked you? I kept waiting. We could talk everything over there.

LARRY

There's nothing to talk over!

PARRITT

But I've got to talk to you. Or I'll talk to Hickey. He won't let me alone! I feel he knows, anyway! And I know he'd understand, all right—in his way. But I hate his guts! I don't want anything to do with him! I'm scared of him, honest. There's something not human behind his damned grinning and kidding.

LARRY
Starts.
Ah! You feel that, too?

PARRITT
Pleadingly.
But I can't go on like this. I've got to decide what I've got to do. I've got to tell you, Larry!

LARRY
Again starts up.
I won't listen!

PARRITT
Again holds him by the arm.
All right! I won't. Don't go!
LARRY *lets himself be pulled down on his chair.* PARRITT *examines his face and becomes insultingly scornful.*
Who do you think you're kidding? I know damned well you've guessed—

LARRY
I've guessed nothing!

PARRITT
But I want you to guess now! I'm glad you have! I know now, since Hickey's been after me, that I meant you to guess right from the start. That's why I came to you.
Hurrying on with an attempt at a plausible frank air that makes what he says seem doubly false.
I want you to understand the reason. You see, I began studying American history. I got admiring Washington and Jefferson and Jackson and Lincoln. I began to feel patriotic and love this country. I saw it was the best government in the world, where everybody was equal and had a chance. I saw that all the ideas behind the Movement came from a lot of Russians like Bakunin and Kropotkin and were meant for Europe, but we didn't need them here in a democ-

racy where we were free already. I didn't want this country to be destroyed for a damned foreign pipe dream. After all, I'm from old American pioneer stock. I began to feel I was a traitor for helping a lot of cranks and bums and free women plot to overthrow our government. And then I saw it was my duty to my country—

LARRY

Nauseated—turns on him.
You stinking rotten liar! Do you think you can fool me with such hypocrite's cant!
Then turning away.
I don't give a damn what you did! It's on your head—whatever it was! I don't want to know—and I won't know!

PARRITT

As if LARRY *had never spoken—falteringly.*
But I never thought Mother would be caught. Please believe that, Larry. You know I never would have—

LARRY

His face haggard, drawing a deep breath and closing his eyes—as if he were trying to hammer something into his own brain.
All I know is I'm sick of life! I'm through! I've forgotten myself! I'm drowned and contented on the bottom of a bottle. Honor or dishonor, faith or treachery are nothing to me but the opposites of the same stupidity which is ruler and king of life, and in the end they rot into dust in the same grave. All things are the same meaningless joke to me, for they grin at me from the one skull of death. So go away. You're wasting breath. I've forgotten your mother.

PARRITT

Jeers angrily.
The old foolosopher, eh?
He spits out contemptuously.
You lousy old faker!

LARRY

So distracted he pleads weakly.
For the love of God, leave me in peace the little time that's left to me!

PARRITT

Aw, don't pull that pitiful old-man junk on me! You old bastard, you'll never die as long as there's a free drink of whiskey left!

LARRY

Stung—furiously.

Look out how you try to taunt me back into life, I warn you! I might remember the thing they call justice there, and the punishment for—

He checks himself with an effort—then with a real indifference that comes from exhaustion.

I'm old and tired. To hell with you! You're as mad as Hickey, and as big a liar. I'd never let myself believe a word you told me.

PARRITT

Threateningly.

The hell you won't! Wait till Hickey gets through with you!

PEARL *and* MARGIE *come in from the bar. At the sight of them,* PAR-RITT *instantly subsides and becomes self-conscious and defensive, scowling at them and then quickly looking away.*

MARGIE

Eyes him jeeringly.

Why, hello, Tightwad Kid. Come to join de party? Gee, don't he act bashful, Poil?

PEARL

Yeah. Especially wid his dough.

PARRITT *slinks to a chair at the left end of the table, pretending he hasn't heard them. Suddenly there is a noise of angry, cursing voices and a scuffle from the hall.* PEARL *yells.*

Hey, Rocky! Fight in de hall!

ROCKY *and* CHUCK *run from behind the bar curtain and rush into the hall.* ROCKY'S *voice is heard in irritated astonishment, "What de hell?" and then the scuffle stops and* ROCKY *appears holding* CAPTAIN LEWIS *by the arm, followed by* CHUCK *with a similar hold on* GEN-ERAL WETJOEN. *Although these two have been drinking they are both sober, for them. Their faces are sullenly angry, their clothes disarranged from the tussle.*

ROCKY
Leading LEWIS *forward—astonished, amused and irritated.*
Can yuh beat it? I've heard youse two call each odder every name
yuh could think of but I never seen you—
Indignantly.
A swell time to stage your first bout, on Harry's boithday party!
What started de scrap?

LEWIS
Forcing a casual tone.
Nothing, old chap. Our business, you know. That bloody ass,
Hickey, made some insinuation about me, and the boorish Boer had
the impertinence to agree with him.

WETJOEN
Dot's a lie! Hickey made joke about me, and this Limey said yes, it
was true!

ROCKY
Well, sit down, de bot' of yuh, and cut out de rough stuff.
He and CHUCK *dump them down in adjoining chairs toward the left
end of the table, where, like two sulky boys, they turn their backs on each
other as far as possible in chairs which both face front.*

MARGIE
Laughs.
Jees, lookit de two bums! Like a coupla kids! Kiss and make up, for
Gawd's sakes!

ROCKY
Yeah. Harry's party begins in a minute and we don't want no sore-
heads around.

LEWIS
Stiffly.
Very well. In deference to the occasion, I apologize, General Wetjoen
—provided that you do also.

WETJOEN
Sulkily.

I apologize, Captain Lewis—because Harry is my goot friend.

ROCKY

Aw, hell! If yuh can't do better'n dat—!

MOSHER *and* MCGLOIN *enter together from the hall. Both have been drinking but are not drunk.*

PEARL

Here's de star boarders.

They advance, their heads together, so interested in a discussion they are oblivious to everyone.

MCGLOIN

I'm telling you, Ed, it's serious this time. That bastard, Hickey, has got Harry on the hip.

As he talks, MARGIE, PEARL, ROCKY *and* CHUCK *prick up their ears and gather round.* CORA, *at the piano, keeps running through the tune, with soft pedal, and singing the chorus half under her breath, with* JOE *still correcting her mistakes. At the table,* LARRY, PARRITT, WILLIE, WETJOEN *and* LEWIS *sit motionless, staring in front of them.* HUGO *seems asleep in his habitual position.*

And you know it isn't going to do us no good if he gets him to take that walk tomorrow.

MOSHER

You're damned right. Harry'll mosey around the ward, dropping in on everyone who knew him when.

Indignantly.

And they'll all give him a phony glad hand and a ton of good advice about what a sucker he is to stand for us.

MCGLOIN

He's sure to call on Bessie's relations to do a little cryin' over dear Bessie. And you know what that bitch and all her family thought of me.

MOSHER

With a flash of his usual humor—rebukingly.

Remember, Lieutenant, you are speaking of my sister! Dear Bessie wasn't a bitch. She was a God-damned bitch! But if you think my loving relatives will have time to discuss you, you don't know them. They'll be too busy telling Harry what a drunken crook I am and saying he ought to have me put in Sing Sing!

MCGLOIN
Dejectedly.
Yes, once Bessie's relations get their hooks in him, it'll be as tough for us as if she wasn't gone.

MOSHER
Dejectedly.
Yes, Harry has always been weak and easily influenced, and now he's getting old he'll be an easy mark for those grafters.
Then with forced reassurance.
Oh, hell, Mac, we're saps to worry. We've heard Harry pull that bluff about taking a walk every birthday he's had for twenty years.

MCGLOIN
Doubtfully.
But Hickey wasn't sicking him on those times. Just the opposite. He was asking Harry what he wanted to go out for when there was plenty of whiskey here.

MOSHER
With a change to forced carelessness.
Well, after all, I don't care whether he goes out or not. I'm clearing out tomorrow morning anyway. I'm just sorry for you, Mac.

MCGLOIN
Resentfully.
You needn't be, then. Ain't I going myself? I was only feeling sorry for you.

MOSHER
Yes, my mind is made up. Hickey may be a lousy, interfering pest, now he's gone teetotal on us, but there's a lot of truth in some of his bull. Hanging around here getting plastered with you, Mac, is pleasant, I won't deny, but the old booze gets you in the end, if you keep lapping it up. It's time I quit for a while.
With forced enthusiasm.

Besides, I feel the call of the old carefree circus life in my blood again. I'll see the boss tomorrow. It's late in the season but he'll be glad to take me on. And won't all the old gang be tickled to death when I show up on the lot!

MCGLOIN

Maybe—if they've got a rope handy!

MOSHER

Turns on him—angrily.
Listen! I'm damned sick of that kidding!

MCGLOIN

You are, are you? Well, I'm sicker of your kidding me about getting reinstated on the Force. And whatever you'd like, I can't spend my life sitting here with you, ruining my stomach with rotgut. I'm tapering off, and in the morning I'll be fresh as a daisy. I'll go and have a private chin with the Commissioner.
With forced enthusiasm.
Man alive, from what the boys tell me, there's sugar galore these days, and I'll soon be ridin' around in a big red automobile—

MOSHER

Derisively—beckoning an imaginary Chinese.
Here, One Lung Hop! Put fresh peanut oil in the lamp and cook the Lieutenant another dozen pills! It's his gowed-up night!

MCGLOIN

Stung—pulls back a fist threateningly.
One more crack like that and I'll—!

MOSHER

Putting up his fists.
Yes? Just start—!
CHUCK *and* ROCKY *jump between them.*

ROCKY

Hey! Are you guys nuts? Jees, it's Harry's boithday party!
They both look guilty.
Sit down and behave.

MOSHER

Grumpily.

All right. Only tell him to lay off me.

He lets ROCKY *push him in a chair, at the right end of the table, rear.*

MCGLOIN

Grumpily.

Tell him to lay off me.

He lets CHUCK *push him into the chair on* MOSHER'S *left. At this moment* HICKEY *bursts in from the hall, bustling and excited.*

HICKEY

Everything all set? Fine!

He glances at his watch.

Half a minute to go. Harry's starting down with Jimmy. I had a hard time getting them to move! They'd rather stay hiding up there, kidding each other along.

He chuckles.

Harry don't even want to remember its his birthday now!

He hears a noise from the stairs.

Here they come!

Urgently.

Light the candles! Get ready to play, Cora! Stand up, everybody! Get that wine ready, Chuck and Rocky!

MARGIE *and* PEARL *light the candles on the cake.* CORA *gets her hands set over the piano keys, watching over her shoulder.* ROCKY *and* CHUCK *go in the bar. Everybody at the table stands up mechanically.* HUGO *is the last, suddenly coming to and scrambling to his feet.* HARRY HOPE *and* JIMMY TOMORROW *appear in the hall outside the door.* HICKEY *looks up from his watch.*

On the dot! It's twelve!

Like a cheer leader.

Come on now, everybody, with a Happy Birthday, Harry!

With his voice leading they all shout "Happy Birthday Harry!" in a spiritless chorus. HICKEY *signals to* CORA, *who starts playing and singing in a whiskey soprano "She's the Sunshine of Paradise Alley."* HOPE *and* JIMMY *stand in the doorway. Both have been drinking heavily. In* HOPE *the effect is apparent only in a bristling, touchy, pugnacious atti-*

*tude. It is entirely different from the usual irascible beefing he delights in
and which no one takes seriously. Now he really has a chip on his shoulder.* JIMMY, *on the other hand, is plainly drunk, but it has not had the
desired effect, for beneath a pathetic assumption of gentlemanly poise,
he is obviously frightened and shrinking back within himself.* HICKEY
grabs HOPE'S *hand and pumps it up and down. For a moment* HOPE
*appears unconscious of this handshake. Then he jerks his hand away an-
grily.*

HOPE

Cut out the glad hand, Hickey. D'you think I'm a sucker? I know
you, bejees, you sneaking, lying drummer!
With rising anger, to the others.
And all you bums! What the hell you trying to do, yelling and raising
the roof? Want the cops to close the joint and get my license taken
away?
He yells at CORA *who has stopped singing but continues to play mechanically with many mistakes.*
Hey, you dumb tart, quit banging that box! Bejees, the least you
could do is learn the tune!

CORA

Stops—deeply hurt.
Aw, Harry! Jees, ain't I—
Her eyes begin to fill.

HOPE

Glaring at the other girls.
And you two hookers, screaming at the top of your lungs! What
d'you think this is, a dollar cathouse? Bejees, that's where you belong!

PEARL

Miserably.
Aw, Harry—
She begins to cry.

MARGIE

Jees, Harry, I never thought you'd say that—like yuh meant it.

She puts her arm around PEARL — *on the verge of tears herself.*
Aw, don't bawl, Poil. He don't mean it.

HICKEY
Reproachfully.
Now, Harry! Don't take it out on the gang because you're upset about yourself. Anyway, I've promised you you'll come through all right, haven't I? So quit worrying.
He slaps HOPE *on the back encouragingly.* HOPE *flashes him a glance of hate.*
Be yourself, Governor. You don't want to bawl out the old gang just when they're congratulating you on your birthday, do you? Hell, that's no way!

HOPE
Looking guilty and shamefaced now — forcing an unconvincing attempt at his natural tone.
Bejees, they ain't as dumb as you. They know I was only kidding them. They know I appreciate their congratulations. Don't you, fellers?
There is a listless chorus of "Sure, Harry," "Yes," "Of course we do," etc. He comes forward to the two girls, with JIMMY *and* HICKEY *following him, and pats them clumsily.*
Bejees, I like you broads. You know I was only kidding.
Instantly they forgive him and smile affectionately.

MARGIE
Sure we know, Harry.

PEARL
Sure.

HICKEY
Grinning.
Sure. Harry's the greatest kidder in this dump and that's saying something! Look how he's kidded himself for twenty years!
As HOPE *gives him a bitter, angry glance, he digs him in the ribs with his elbow playfully.*

Unless I'm wrong, Governor, and I'm betting I'm not. We'll soon know, eh? Tomorrow morning. No, by God, it's *this* morning now!

JIMMY
With a dazed dread.
This morning?

HICKEY
Yes, it's today at last, Jimmy.
He pats him on the back.
Don't be so scared! I've promised I'll help you.

JIMMY
Trying to hide his dread behind an offended, drunken dignity.
I don't understand you. Kindly remember I'm fully capable of settling my own affairs!

HICKEY
Earnestly.
Well, isn't that exactly what I want you to do, settle with yourself once and for all?
He speaks in his ear in confidential warning.
Only watch out on the booze, Jimmy. You know, not too much from now on. You've had a lot already, and you don't want to let yourself duck out of it by being too drunk to move—not this time!
JIMMY *gives him a guilty, stricken look and turns away and slumps into the chair on* MOSHER's *right.*

HOPE
To MARGIE—*still guiltily.*
Bejees, Margie, you know I didn't mean it. It's that lousy drummer riding me that's got my goat.

MARGIE
I know.
She puts a protecting arm around HOPE *and turns him to face the table with the cake and presents.*
Come on. You ain't noticed your cake yet. Ain't it grand?

HOPE

Trying to brighten up.

Say, that's pretty. Ain't ever had a cake since Bessie— Six candles. Each for ten years, eh? Bejees, that's thoughtful of you.

PEARL

It was Hickey got it.

HOPE

His tone forced.

Well, it was thoughtful of him. He means well, I guess.

His eyes, fixed on the cake, harden angrily.

To hell with his cake.

He starts to turn away. PEARL *grabs his arm.*

PEARL

Wait, Harry. Yuh ain't seen de presents from Margie and me and Cora and Chuck and Rocky. And dere's a watch all engraved wid your name and de date from Hickey.

HOPE

To hell with it! Bejees, he can keep it!

This time he does turn away.

PEARL

Jees, he ain't even goin' to look at our presents.

MARGIE

Bitterly.

Dis is all wrong. We gotta put some life in dis party or I'll go nuts! Hey, Cora, what's de matter wid dat box? Can't yuh play for Harry? Yuh don't have to stop just because he kidded yuh!

HOPE

Rouses himself—with forced heartiness.

Yes, come on, Cora. You was playing it fine.

CORA *begins to play half-heartedly.* HOPE *suddenly becomes almost tearfully sentimental.*

It was Bessie's favorite tune. She was always singing it. It brings her back. I wish—

He chokes up.

HICKEY
Grins at him—amusedly.
Yes, we've all heard you tell us you thought the world of her, Governor.

HOPE
Looks at him with frightened suspicion.
Well, so I did, bejees! Everyone knows I did!
Threateningly.
Bejees, if you say I didn't—

HICKEY
Soothingly.
Now, Governor. I didn't say anything. You're the only one knows the truth about that.
HOPE *stares at him confusedly.* CORA *continues to play. For a moment there is a pause, broken by* JIMMY TOMORROW *who speaks with muzzy, self-pitying melancholy out of a sentimental dream.*

JIMMY
Marjorie's favorite song was "Loch Lomond." She was beautiful and she played the piano beautifully and she had a beautiful voice.
With gentle sorrow.
You were lucky, Harry. Bessie died. But there are more bitter sorrows than losing the woman one loves by the hand of death—

HICKEY
With an amused wink at HOPE.
Now, listen, Jimmy, you needn't go on. We've all heard that story about how you came back to Cape Town and found her in the hay with a staff officer. We know you like to believe that was what started you on the booze and ruined your life.

JIMMY
Stammers.
I—I'm talking to Harry. Will you kindly keep out of—
With a pitiful defiance.
My life is not ruined!

HICKEY

Ignoring this—with a kidding grin.

But I'll bet when you admit the truth to yourself, you'll confess you were pretty sick of her hating you for getting drunk. I'll bet you were really damned relieved when she gave you such a good excuse.

JIMMY *stares at him strickenly.* HICKEY *pats him on the back again—with sincere sympathy.*

I know how it is, Jimmy. I—

He stops abruptly and for a second he seems to lose his self-assurance and become confused.

LARRY

Seizing on this with vindictive relish.

Ha! So that's what happened to you, is it? Your iceman joke finally came home to roost, did it?

He grins tauntingly.

You should have remembered there's truth in the old superstition that you'd better look out what you call because in the end it comes to you!

HICKEY

Himself again—grins to LARRY *kiddingly.*

Is that a fact, Larry? Well, well! Then you'd better watch out how you keep calling for that old Big Sleep!

LARRY *starts and for a second looks superstitiously frightened. Abruptly* HICKEY *changes to his jovial, bustling, master-of-ceremonies manner.*

But what are we waiting for, boys and girls? Let's start the party rolling!

He shouts to the bar.

Hey, Chuck and Rocky! Bring on the big surprise! Governor, you sit at the head of the table here.

He makes HARRY *sit down on the chair at the end of the table, right.*

To MARGIE *and* PEARL.

Come on, girls, sit down.

They sit side by side on JIMMY's *right.* HICKEY *bustles down to the left end of table.*

I'll sit here at the foot.

He sits, with CORA *on his left and* JOE *on her left.* ROCKY *and* CHUCK *appear from the bar, each bearing a big tray laden with schooners of champagne which they start shoving in front of each member of the party.*

ROCKY
With forced cheeriness.
Real champagne, bums! Cheer up! What is dis, a funeral? Jees, mixin' champagne wid Harry's redeye will knock yuh paralyzed! Ain't yuh never satisfied?
He and CHUCK *finish serving out the schooners, grab the last two them-selves and sit down in the two vacant chairs remaining near the middle of the table. As they do so,* HICKEY *rises, a schooner in his hand.*

HICKEY
Rapping on the table for order when there is nothing but a dead silence.
Order! Order, Ladies and Gents!
He catches LARRY's *eyes on the glass in his hand.*
Yes, Larry, I'm going to drink with you this time. To prove I'm not teetotal because I'm afraid booze would make me spill my secrets, as you think.
LARRY *looks sheepish.* HICKEY *chuckles and goes on.*
No, I gave you the simple truth about that. I don't need booze or anything else any more. But I want to be sociable and propose a toast in honor of our old friend, Harry, and drink it with you.
His eyes fix on HUGO, *who is out again, his head on his plate— To* CHUCK, *who is on* HUGO's *left.*
Wake up our demon bomb-tosser, Chuck. We don't want corpses at this feast.

CHUCK
Gives HUGO *a shake.*
Hey, Hugo, come up for air! Don't yuh see de champagne?
HUGO *blinks around and giggles foolishly.*

HUGO
Ve vill eat birthday cake and trink champagne beneath the villow tree!
He grabs his schooner and takes a greedy gulp—then sets it back on the

table with a grimace of distance—in a strange, arrogantly disdainful tone, as if he were rebuking a butler.

Dis vine is unfit to trink. It has not properly been iced.

HICKEY
Amusedly.

Always a high-toned swell at heart, eh, Hugo? God help us poor bums if you'd ever get to telling us where to get off! You'd have been drinking our blood beneath those willow trees!

He chuckles. HUGO *shrinks back in his chair, blinking at him, but* HICKEY *is now looking up the table at* HOPE. *He starts his toast, and as he goes on he becomes more moved and obviously sincere.*

Here's the toast, Ladies and Gents! Here's to Harry Hope, who's been a friend in need to every one of us! Here's to the old Governor, the best sport and the kindest, biggest-hearted guy in the world! Here's wishing you all the luck there is, Harry, and long life and happiness! Come on, everybody! To Harry! Bottoms up!

They have all caught his sincerity with eager relief. They raise their schooners with an enthusiastic chorus of "Here's how, Harry!" "Here's luck, Harry!" etc., and gulp half the wine down, HICKEY *leading them in this.*

HOPE
Deeply moved—his voice husky.

Bejees, thanks, all of you. Bejees, Hickey, you old son of a bitch, that's white of you! Bejees, I know you meant it, too.

HICKEY
Moved.

Of course I meant it, Harry, old friend! And I mean it when I say I hope today will be the biggest day in your life, and in the lives of everyone here, the beginning of a new life of peace and contentment where no pipe dream can ever nag at you again. Here's to that, Harry!

He drains the remainder of his drink, but this time he drinks alone. In an instant the attitude of everyone has reverted to uneasy, suspicious defensiveness.

ROCKY

Growls.

Aw, forget dat bughouse line of bull for a minute, can't yuh?

HICKEY

Sitting down — good-naturedly.

You're right, Rocky, I'm talking too much. It's Harry we want to hear from. Come on, Harry!

He pounds his schooner on the table.

Speech! Speech!

They try to recapture their momentary enthusiasm, rap their schooners on the table, call "Speech," but there is a hollow ring in it. HOPE *gets to his feet reluctantly, with a forced smile, a smoldering resentment beginning to show in his manner.*

HOPE

Lamely.

Bejees, I'm no good at speeches. All I can say is thanks to everybody again for remembering me on my birthday.

Bitterness coming out.

Only don't think because I'm sixty I'll be a bigger damned fool easy mark than ever! No, bejees! Like Hickey says, it's going to be a new day! This dump has got to be run like other dumps, so I can make some money and not just split even. People has got to pay what they owe me! I'm not running a damned orphan asylum for bums and crooks! Nor a God-damned hooker shanty, either! Nor an Old Men's Home for lousy Anarchist tramps that ought to be in jail! I'm sick of being played for a sucker!

They stare at him with stunned, bewildered hurt. He goes on in a sort of furious desperation, as if he hated himself for every word he said, and yet couldn't stop.

And don't think you're kidding me right now, either! I know damned well you're giving me the laugh behind my back, thinking to yourselves, The old, lying, pipe-dreaming faker, we've heard his bull about taking a walk around the ward for years, he'll never make it! He's yellow, he ain't got the guts, he's scared he'll find out —

He glares around at them almost with hatred.

But I'll show you, bejees!

127

He glares at HICKEY.

I'll show you, too, you son of a bitch of a frying-pan-peddling bastard!

HICKEY

Heartily encouraging.

That's the stuff, Harry! Of course you'll try to show me! That's what I want you to do!

HARRY *glances at him with helpless dread—then drops his eyes and looks furtively around the table. All at once he becomes miserably contrite.*

HOPE

His voice catching.

Listen, all of you! Bejees, forgive me. I lost my temper! I ain't feeling well! I got a hell of a grouch on! Bejees, you know you're all as welcome here as the flowers in May!

They look at him with eager forgiveness. ROCKY *is the first one who can voice it.*

ROCKY

Aw, sure, Boss, you're always aces wid us, see?

HICKEY

Rises to his feet again. He addresses them now with the simple, convincing sincerity of one making a confession of which he is genuinely ashamed.

Listen, everybody! I know you are sick of my gabbing, but I think this is the spot where I owe it to you to do a little explaining and apologize for some of the rough stuff I've had to pull on you. I know how it must look to you. As if I was a damned busybody who was not only interfering in your private business, but even sicking some of you on to nag at each other. Well, I have to admit that's true, and I'm damned sorry about it. But it simply had to be done! You must believe that! You know old Hickey. I was never one to start trouble. But this time I had to—for your own good! I had to make you help me with each other. I saw I couldn't do what I was after alone. Not in the time at my disposal. I knew when I came here I wouldn't be able to stay with you long. I'm slated to leave on a trip. I saw I'd have to hustle and use every means I could.

With a joking boastfulness.

Why, if I had enough time, I'd get a lot of sport out of selling my line of salvation to each of you all by my lonesome. Like it was fun in the old days, when I traveled house to house, to convince some dame, who was sicking the dog on me, her house wouldn't be properly furnished unless she bought another wash boiler. And I could do it with you, all right. I know every one of you, inside and out, by heart. I may have been drunk when I've been here before, but old Hickey could never be so drunk he didn't have to see through people. I mean, everyone except himself. And, finally, he had to see through himself, too.

He pauses. They stare at him, bitter, uneasy and fascinated. His manner changes to deep earnestness.

But here's the point to get. I swear I'd never act like I have if I wasn't absolutely sure it will be worth it to you in the end, after you're rid of the damned guilt that makes you lie to yourselves you're something you're not, and the remorse that nags at you and makes you hide behind lousy pipe dreams about tomorrow. You'll be in a today where there is no yesterday or tomorrow to worry you. You won't give a damn what you are any more. I wouldn't say this unless I knew, Brothers and Sisters. This peace is real! It's a fact! I know! Because I've got it! Here! Now! Right in front of you! You see the difference in me! You remember how I used to be! Even when I had two quarts of rotgut under my belt and joked and sang "Sweet Adeline," I still felt like a guilty skunk. But you can all see that I don't give a damn about anything now. And I promise you, by the time this day is over, I'll have every one of you feeling the same way!

He pauses. They stare at him fascinatedly. He adds with a grin.

I guess that'll be about all from me, boys and girls—for the present. So let's get on with the party.

He starts to sit down.

LARRY

Sharply.

Wait!

Insistently—with a sneer.

I think it would help us poor pipe-dreaming sinners along the sawdust trail to salvation if you told us now what it was happened to you that converted you to this great peace you've found.

More and more with a deliberate, provocative taunting.

I notice you didn't deny it when I asked you about the iceman. Did this great revelation of the evil habit of dreaming about tomorrow come to you after you found your wife was sick of you?

While he is speaking the faces of the gang have lighted up vindictively, as if all at once they saw a chance to revenge themselves. As he finishes, a chorus of sneering taunts begins, punctuated by nasty, jeering laughter.

HOPE

Bejees, you've hit it, Larry! I've noticed he hasn't shown her picture around this time!

MOSHKER

He hasn't got it! The iceman took it away from him!

MARGIE

Jees, look at him! Who could blame her?

PEARL

She must be hard up to fall for an iceman!

CORA

Imagine a sap like him advisin' me and Chuck to git married!

CHUCK

Yeah! He done so good wid it!

JIMMY

At least I can say Marjorie chose an officer and a gentleman.

LEWIS

Come to look at you, Hickey, old chap, you've sprouted horns like a bloody antelope!

WETJOEN

Pigger, py Gott! Like a water buffalo's!

WILLIE

Sings to his Sailor Lad tune.

   "Come up," she cried, "my iceman lad,

And you and I'll agree—"
They all join in a jeering chorus, rapping with knuckles or glasses on the table at the indicated spot in the lyric.

"And I'll show you the prettiest

Rap, rap, rap.

That ever you did see!"

A roar of derisive, dirty laughter. But HICKEY *has remained unmoved by all this taunting. He grins good-naturedly, as if he enjoyed the joke at his expense, and joins in the laughter.*

HICKEY

Well, boys and girls, I'm glad to see you getting in good spirits for Harry's party, even if the joke is on me. I admit I asked for it by always pulling that iceman gag in the old days. So laugh all you like.
He pauses. They do not laugh now. They are again staring at him with baffled uneasiness. He goes on thoughtfully.

Well, this forces my hand, I guess, your bringing up the subject of Evelyn. I didn't want to tell you yet. It's hardly an appropriate time. I meant to wait until the party was over. But you're getting the wrong idea about poor Evelyn, and I've got to stop that.
He pauses again. There is a tense stillness in the room. He bows his head a little and says quietly.

I'm sorry to tell you my dearly beloved wife is dead.
A gasp comes from the stunned company. They look away from him, shocked and miserably ashamed of themselves, except LARRY *who continues to stare at him.*

LARRY

Aloud to himself with a superstitious shrinking.

Be God, I felt he'd brought the touch of death on him!
Then suddenly he is even more ashamed of himself than the others and stammers.

Forgive me, Hickey! I'd like to cut my dirty tongue out!
This releases a chorus of shamefaced mumbles from the crowd. "Sorry, Hickey." "I'm sorry, Hickey." "We're sorry, Hickey."

HICKEY

Looking around at them—in a kindly, reassuring tone.

Now look here, everybody. You mustn't let this be a wet blanket on Harry's party. You're still getting me all wrong. There's no reason— You see, I don't feel any grief.

They gaze at him startledly. He goes on with convincing sincerity.

I've got to feel glad, for her sake. Because she's at peace. She's rid of me at last. Hell, I don't have to tell you—you all know what I was like. You can imagine what she went through, married to a no-good cheater and drunk like I was. And there was no way out of it for her. Because she loved me. But now she is at peace like she always longed to be. So why should I feel sad? She wouldn't want me to feel sad. Why, all that Evelyn ever wanted out of life was to make me happy. *He stops, looking around at them with a simple, gentle frankness. They stare at him in bewildered, incredulous confusion.*

CURTAIN

Act Three

SCENE

Barroom of HARRY HOPE'S, *including a part of what had been the back room in Acts One and Two. In the right wall are two big windows, with the swinging doors to the street between them. The bar itself is at rear. Behind it is a mirror, covered with white mosquito netting to keep off the flies, and a shelf on which are barrels of cheap whiskey with spiggots and a small show case of bottled goods. At left of the bar is the doorway to the hall. There is a table at left, front, of barroom proper, with four chairs. At right, front, is a small free-lunch counter, facing left, with a space between it and the window for the dealer to stand when he dishes out soup at the noon hour. Over the mirror behind the bar are framed photographs of Richard Croker and Big Tim Sullivan, flanked by framed lithographs of John L. Sullivan and Gentleman Jim Corbett in ring costume.*

At left, in what had been the back room, with the dividing curtain drawn, the banquet table of Act Two has been broken up, and the tables are again in the crowded arrangement of Act One. Of these, we see one in the front row with five chairs at left of the barroom table, another with five chairs at left-rear of it, a third back by the rear wall with five chairs, and finally, at extreme left-front, one with four chairs, partly on and partly off stage, left.

It is around the middle of the morning of HOPE'S *birthday, a hot summer day. There is sunlight in the street outside, but it does not hit the windows and the light in the back-room section is dim.*

JOE MOTT *is moving around, a box of sawdust under his arm, strewing it over the floor. His manner is sullen, his face set in gloom. He ignores everyone. As the scene progresses, he finishes his sawdusting job, goes behind the lunch counter and cuts loaves of bread.* ROCKY *is behind the bar, wiping it, washing glasses, etc. He wears his working clothes, sleeves rolled up. He looks sleepy, irritable and worried. At the barroom table, front,* LARRY *sits in a chair, facing right-front. He has no drink in front of him. He stares ahead, deep in harried thought. On his right, in a chair facing right,* HUGO *sits sprawled forward, arms and head on the table as usual, a whiskey glass beside his limp hand. At rear of the front table at left of them, in a chair facing left,* PARRITT *is sitting. He is staring in front of him in a tense, strained immobility.*

As the curtain rises, ROCKY *finishes his work behind the bar. He comes forward and drops wearily in the chair at right of* LARRY'S *table, facing left.*

ROCKY

Nuttin' now till de noon rush from de Market. I'm goin' to rest my fanny.

Irritably.

If I ain't a sap to let Chuck kid me into workin' his time so's he can take de mornin' off. But I got sick of arguin' wid 'im. I says, "Aw right, git married! What's it to me?" Hickey's got de bot' of dem bugs.

Bitterly.

Some party last night, huh? Jees, what a funeral! It was jinxed from de start, but his tellin' about his wife croakin' put de K.O. on it.

LARRY

Yes, it turned out it wasn't a birthday feast but a wake!

ROCKY

Him promisin' he'd cut out de bughouse bull about peace—and den he went on talkin' and talkin' like he couldn't stop! And all de gang sneakin' upstairs, leavin' free booze and eats like dey was poison! It didn't do dem no good if dey thought dey'd shake him. He's been hoppin' from room to room all night. Yuh can't stop him. He's got his Reform Wave goin' strong dis mornin'! Did yuh notice him drag Jimmy out de foist ting to get his laundry and his clothes pressed so he wouldn't have no excuse? And he give Willie de dough to buy his stuff back from Solly's. And all de rest been brushin' and shavin' demselves wid de shakes—

LARRY
Defiantly.
He didn't come to my room! He's afraid I might ask him a few questions.

ROCKY
Scornfully.
Yeah? It don't look to me he's scared of yuh. I'd say you was scared of him.

LARRY
Stung.
You'd lie, then!

PARRITT
Jerks round to look at LARRY—*sneeringly.*
Don't let him kid you, Rocky. He had his door locked. I couldn't get in, either.

ROCKY
Yeah, who d'yuh tink yuh're kiddin', Larry? He's showed you up, aw right. Like he says, if yuh was so anxious to croak, why wouldn't yuh hop off your fire escape long ago?

LARRY
Defiantly.
Because it'd be a coward's quitting, that's why!

PARRITT
He's all quitter, Rocky. He's a yellow old faker!

LARRY
Turns on him.
You lying punk! Remember what I warned you—!

ROCKY
Scowls at PARRITT.
Yeah, keep outta dis, you! Where d'yuh get license to butt in? Shall

I give him de bum's rush, Larry? If you don't want him around, nobody else don't.

LARRY
Forcing an indifferent tone.
No. Let him stay. I don't mind him. He's nothing to me.
ROCKY *shrugs his shoulders and yawns sleepily.*

PARRITT
You're right, I have nowhere to go now. You're the only one in the world I can turn to.

ROCKY
Drowsily.
Yuh're a soft old sap, Larry. He's a no-good louse like Hickey. He don't belong.
He yawns.
I'm all in. Not a wink of sleep. Can't keep my peepers open.
His eyes close and his head nods. PARRITT *gives him a glance and then gets up and slinks over to slide into the chair on* LARRY's *left, between him and* ROCKY. LARRY *shrinks away, but determinedly ignores him.*

PARRITT
Bending toward him — in a low, ingratiating, apologetic voice.
I'm sorry for riding you, Larry. But you get my goat when you act as if you didn't care a damn what happened to me, and keep you door locked so I can't talk to you.
Then hopefully.
But that was to keep Hickey out, wasn't it? I don't blame you. I'm getting to hate him. I'm getting more and more scared of him. Especially since he told us his wife was dead. It's that queer feeling he gives me that I'm mixed up with him some way. I don't know why, but it started me thinking about Mother — as if she was dead.
With a strange undercurrent of something like satisfaction in his pitying tone.
I suppose she might as well be. Inside herself, I mean. It must kill her when she thinks of me — I know she doesn't want to, but she can't help it. After all, I'm her only kid. She used to spoil me and made a pet of me. Once in a great while, I mean. When she remembered

me. As if she wanted to make up for something. As if she felt guilty. So she must have loved me a little, even if she never let it interfere with her freedom.

With a strange pathetic wistfulness.

Do you know, Larry, I once had a sneaking suspicion that maybe, if the truth was known, you were my father.

LARRY

Violently.

You damned fool! Who put that insane idea in your head? You know it's a lie! Anyone in the Coast crowd could tell you I never laid eyes on your mother till after you were born.

PARRITT

Well, I'd hardly ask them, would I? I know you're right, though, because I asked her. She brought me up to be frank and ask her anything, and she'd always tell me the truth.

Abruptly.

But I was talking about how she must feel now about me. My getting through with the Movement. She'll never forgive that. The Movement is her life. And it must be the final knockout for her if she knows I was the one who sold—

LARRY

Shut up, damn you!

PARRITT

It'll kill her. And I'm sure she knows it must have been me.

Suddenly with desperate urgency.

But I never thought the cops would get her! You've got to believe that! You've got to see what my only reason was! I'll admit what I told you last night was a lie—that bunk about getting patriotic and my duty to my country. But here's the true reason, Larry—the only reason! It was just for money! I got stuck on a whore and wanted dough to blow in on her and have a good time! That's all I did it for! Just money! Honest.

He has the terrible grotesque air, in confessing his sordid baseness, of one who gives an excuse which exonerates him from any real guilt.

LARRY

Grabs him by the shoulder and shakes him.

God damn you, shut up! What the hell is it to me?

ROCKY *starts awake.*

ROCKY

What's comin' off here?

LARRY

Controlling himself.

Nothing. This gabby young punk was talking my ear off, that's all.
He's a worse pest than Hickey.

ROCKY

Drowsily.

Yeah, Hickey— Say, listen, what d'yuh mean about him bein' scared
you'd ask him questions? What questions?

LARRY

Well, I feel he's hiding something. You notice he didn't say what his
wife died of.

ROCKY

Rebukingly.

Aw, lay off dat. De poor guy— What are yuh gettin' at, anyway? Yuh
don't tink it's just a gag of his?

LARRY

I don't. I'm damned sure he's brought death here with him. I feel the
cold touch of it on him.

ROCKY

Aw, bunk! You got croakin' on de brain, Old Cemetery.

Suddenly ROCKY's *eyes widen.*

Say! D'yuh mean yuh tink she committed suicide, 'count of his
cheatin' or someting?

LARRY

Grimly.

It wouldn't surprise me. I'd be the last to blame her.

ROCKY

Scornfully.

But dat's crazy! Jees, if she'd done dat, he wouldn't tell us he was glad about it, would he? He ain't dat big a bastard.

PARRITT

Speaks up from his own preoccupation—strangely.

You know better than that, Larry. You know she'd never commit suicide. She's like you. She'll hang on to life even when there's nothing left but—

LARRY

Stung—turns on him viciously.

And how about you? Be God, if you had any guts or decency—! *He stops guiltily.*

PARRITT

Sneeringly.

I'd take that hop off your fire escape you're too yellow to take, I suppose?

LARRY

As if to himself.

No! Who am I to judge? I'm done with judging.

PARRITT

Tauntingly.

Yes, I suppose you'd like that, wouldn't you?

ROCKY

Irritably mystified.

What de hell's all dis about?

To PARRITT.

What d'you know about Hickey's wife? How d'yuh know she didn't—?

LARRY

With forced belittling casualness.

He doesn't. Hickey's addled the little brains he's got. Shove him back to his own table, Rocky. I'm sick of him.

ROCKY

To PARRITT, *threateningly.*

Yuh heard Larry? I'd like an excuse to give yuh a good punch in de snoot. So move quick!

PARRITT

Gets up—to LARRY.

If you think moving to another table will get rid of me!

He moves away—then adds with bitter reproach.

Gee, Larry, that's a hell of a way to treat me, when I've trusted you, and I need your help.

He sits down in his old place and sinks into a wounded, self-pitying brooding.

ROCKY

Going back to his train of thought.

Jees, if she committed suicide, yuh got to feel sorry for Hickey, huh? Yuh can understand how he'd go bughouse and not be responsible for all de crazy stunts he's stagin' here.

Then puzzledly.

But how can yuh be sorry for him when he says he's glad she croaked, and yuh can tell he means it?

With weary exasperation.

Aw, nuts! I don't get nowhere tryin' to figger his game.

His face hardening.

But I know dis. He better lay off me and my stable!

He pauses—then sighs.

Jees, Larry, what a night dem two pigs give me! When de party went dead, dey pinched a couple bottles and brung dem up deir room and got stinko. I don't get a wink of sleep, see? Just as I'd drop off on a chair here, dey'd come down lookin' for trouble. Or else dey'd raise hell upstairs, laughin' and singin', so I'd get scared dey'd get de joint pinched and go up to tell dem to can de noise. And every time dey'd crawl my frame wid de same old argument. Dey'd say, "So yuh agreed wid Hickey, do yuh, yuh dirty little Ginny? We're whores, are we? Well, we agree wid Hickey about you, see! Yuh're nuttin' but a lousy pimp!" Den I'd slap dem. Not beat 'em up, like a pimp would. Just slap dem. But it don't do no good. Dey'd keep at it over and over. Jees, I get de earache just thinkin' of it! "Listen," dey'd say, "if we're whores we gotta right to have a reg'lar pimp and not stand for no punk imitation! We're sick of wearin' out our dogs poundin' sidewalks for a double-crossin' bartender, when all de thanks we get is he looks down on us. We'll find a guy who really needs us to take care of him and ain't ashamed of it. Don't expect us to work tonight, 'cause we won't, see? Not if de streets was blocked wid sailors! We're goin' on strike and yuh can like it or lump it!"

He shakes his head.

Whores goin' on strike! Can yuh tie dat?

Going on with his story.

Dey says, "We're takin' a holiday. We're goin' to beat it down to Coney Island and shoot the chutes and maybe we'll come back and maybe we won't. And you can go to hell!" So dey put on deir lids and beat it, de bot' of dem stinko.

He sighs dejectedly. He seems grotesquely like a harried family man, henpecked and browbeaten by a nagging wife. LARRY *is deep in his own bitter preoccupation and hasn't listened to him.* CHUCK *enters from the hall at rear. He has his straw hat with the gaudy band in his hand and wears a Sunday-best blue suit with a high stiff collar. He looks sleepy, hot, uncomfortable and grouchy.*

CHUCK
Glumly.
Hey, Rocky. Cora wants a sherry flip. For her noives.

ROCKY
Turns indignantly.
Sherry flip! Christ, she don't need nuttin' for her noive! What's she tink dis is, de Waldorf?

CHUCK
Yeah, I told her, what would we use for sherry, and dere wasn't no egg unless she laid one. She says, "Is dere a law yuh can't go out and buy de makings, yuh big tramp?"
Resentfully puts his straw hat on his head at a defiant tilt.
To hell wid her! She'll drink booze or nuttin'!
He goes behind the bar to draw a glass of whiskey from a barrel.

ROCKY

Sarcastically.

Jees, a guy oughta give his bride anything she wants on de weddin' day, I should tink!

As CHUCK *comes from behind the bar,* ROCKY *surveys him derisively.*

Pipe de bridegroom, Larry! All dolled up for de killin'!

LARRY *pays no attention.*

CHUCK

Aw, shut up!

ROCKY

One week on dat farm in Joisey, dat's what I give yuh! Yuh'll come runnin' in here some night yellin' for a shot of booze 'cause de crickets is after yuh!

Disgustedly.

Jees, Chuck, dat louse Hickey's coitinly made a prize coupla suckers outa youse.

CHUCK

Unguardedly.

Yeah. I'd like to give him one sock in de puss—just one!

Then angrily.

Aw, can dat! What's he go to do wid it? Ain't we always said we was goin' to? So we're goin' to, see? And don't give me no argument!

He stares at ROCKY *truculently. But* ROCKY *only shrugs his shoulders with weary disgust and* CHUCK *subsides into complaining gloom.*

If on'y Cora'd cut out de beefin'. She don't gimme a minute's rest all night. De same old stuff over and over! Do I really want to marry her? I says, "Sure, Baby, why not?" She says, "Yeah, but after a week yuh'll be tinkin' what a sap you was. Yuh'll make dat an excuse to go off on a periodical, and den I'll be tied for life to a no-good soak, and de foist ting I know yuh'll have me out hustlin' again, your own wife!" Den she'd bust out cryin', and I'd get sore. "Yuh're a liar," I'd say. "I ain't never taken your dough 'cept when I was drunk and not workin'!" "Yeah," she'd say, "and how long will yuh stay sober now? Don't tink yuh can kid me wid dat water-wagon bull! I've heard it too often." Dat'd make me sore and I'd say, "Don't call me a liar.

But I wish I was drunk right now, because if I was, yuh wouldn't be keepin' me awake all night beefin'. If yuh opened your yap, I'd knock de stuffin' outa yuh!" Den she'd yell, "Dat's a sweet way to talk to de goil yuh're goin' to marry."

He sighs explosively.

Jees, she's got me hangin' on de ropes!

He glances with vengeful yearning at the drink of whiskey in his hand.

Jees, would I like to get a quart of dis redeye under my belt!

ROCKY

Well, why de hell don't yuh?

CHUCK

Instantly suspicious and angry.

Sure! You'd like dat, wouldn't yuh? I'm wise to you! Yuh don't wanta see me get married and settle down like a reg'lar guy! Yuh'd like me to stay paralyzed all de time, so's I'd be like you, a lousy pimp!

ROCKY

Springs to his feet, his face hardened viciously.

Listen! I don't take dat even from you, see!

CHUCK

Puts his drink on the bar and clenches his fists.

Yeah? Wanta make sometin' of it?

Jeeringly.

Don't make me laugh! I can lick ten of youse wid one mit!

ROCKY

Reaching for his hip pocket.

Not wid lead in your belly, yuh won't!

JOE

Has stopped cutting when the quarrel started—expostulating.

Hey, you, Rocky and Chuck! Cut it out! You's ole friends! Don't let dat Hickey make you crazy!

CHUCK

Turns on him.

Keep outa our business, yuh black bastard!

ROCKY

Like CHUCK, *turns on* JOE, *as if their own quarrel was forgotten and they became natural allies against an alien.*

Stay where yuh belong, yuh doity nigger!

JOE

Snarling with rage, springs from behind the lunch counter with the bread knife in his hand.

You white sons of bitches! I'll rip your guts out!

CHUCK *snatches a whiskey bottle from the bar and raises is above his head to hurl at* JOE. ROCKY *jerks a short-barreled, nickel-plated revolver from his hip pocket. At this moment* LARRY *pounds on the table with his fist and bursts into a sardonic laugh.*

LARRY

That's it! Murder each other, you damned loons, with Hickey's blessing! Didn't I tell you he'd brought death with him?

His interruption startles them. They pause to stare at him, their fighting fury suddenly dies out and they appear deflated and sheepish.

ROCKY

To JOE.

Aw right, you. Leggo dat shiv and I'll put dis gat away.

JOE *sullenly goes back behind the counter and slaps the knife on top of it.* ROCKY *slips the revolver back in his pocket.* CHUCK *lowers the bottle to the bar.* HUGO, *who has awakened and raised his head when* LARRY *pounded on the table, now giggles foolishly.*

HUGO

Hello, leedle peoples! Neffer mind! Soon you vill eat hot dogs beneath the villow trees and trink free vine—

Abruptly in a haughty fastidious tone.

The champagne vas not properly iced.

With guttural anger.

Gottamned liar, Hickey! Does that prove I vant to be aristocrat? I love only the proletariat! I vill lead them! I vill be like a Gott to them! They vill be my slaves!

He stops in bewildered self-amazement—to LARRY *appealingly.*

I am very trunk, no, Larry? I talk foolishness. I am so trunk, Larry, old friend, am I not, I don't know what I say?

LARRY
Pityingly.
You're raving drunk. Hugo. I've never seen you so paralyzed. Lay your head down now and sleep it off.

HUGO
Gratefully.
Yes. I should sleep. I am too crazy trunk.
He puts his head on his arms and closes his eyes.

JOE
Behind the lunch counter—brooding superstitiously.
You's right, Larry. Bad luck come in de door when Hickey come. I's a old gamblin' man and I knows bad luck when I feels it!
Then defiantly.
But it's white man's bad luck. He can't jinx me!
He comes from behind the counter and goes to the bar—addressing ROCKY *stiffly.*
De bread's cut and I's finished my job. Do I get de drink I's earned?
ROCKY *gives him a hostile look but shoves a bottle and glass at him. Joe pours a brimful drink—sullenly.*
I's finished wid dis dump for keeps.
He takes a key from his pocket and slaps it on the bar.
Here's de key to my room. I ain't comin' back. I's goin' to my own folks where I belong. I don't stay where I's not wanted. I's sick and tired of messin' round wid white men.
He gulps down his drink—then looking around defiantly he deliberately throws his whiskey glass on the floor and smashes it.

ROCKY
Hey! What de hell—!

JOE
With a sneering dignity.
I's on'y savin' you de trouble, White Boy. Now you don't have to break it, soon's my back's turned, so's no white man kick about drinkin' from de same glass.

He walks stiffly to the street door — then turns for a parting shot — boast-fully.

I's tired of loafin' 'round wid a lot of bums. I's a gamblin' man. I's gonna get in a big crap game and win me a big bankroll. Den I'll get de okay to open up my old gamblin' house for colored men. Den maybe I comes back here sometime to see de bums. Maybe I throw a twenty-dollar bill on de bar and say, "Drink it up," and listen when dey all pat me on de back and say, "Joe, you sure is white." But I'll say, "No, I'm black and my dough is black man's dough, and you's proud to drink wid me or you don't get no drink!" Or maybe I just says, "You can all go to hell. I don't lower myself drinkin' wid no white trash!"

He opens the door to go out — then turns again.

And dat ain't no pipe dream! I'll git de money for my stake today, somehow, somewheres! If I has to borrow a gun and stick up some white man, I gets it! You wait and see!

He swaggers out through the swinging doors.

CHUCK

Angrily.

Can yuh beat de noive of dat dinge! Jees, if I wasn't dressed up, I'd go out and mop up de street wid him!

ROCKY

Aw, let him go, de poor old dope! Him and his gamblin' house! He'll be back tonight askin' Harry for his room and bummin' me for a ball.

Vengefully.

Den I'll be de one to smash de glass. I'll loin him his place!

The swinging doors are pushed open and WILLIE OBAN *enters from the street. He is shaved and wears an expensive, well-cut suit, good shoes and clean linen. He is absolutely sober, but his face is sick, and his nerves in a shocking state of shakes.*

CHUCK

Another guy all dolled up! Got your clothes from Solly's, huh, Willie?

Derisively.

Now yuh can sell dem back to him again tomorrow.

WILLIE

Stiffly.

No, I—I'm through with that stuff. Never again.

He comes to the bar.

ROCKY

Sympathetically.

Yuh look sick, Willie. Take a ball to pick yuh up.

He pushes a bottle toward him.

WILLIE

Eyes the bottle yearningly but shakes his head—determinedly.

No, thanks. The only way to stop is to stop. I'd have no chance if I went to the D.A.'s office smelling of booze.

CHUCK

Yuh're really goin' dere?

WILLIE

Stiffly.

I said I was, didn't I? I just came back here to rest a few minutes, not because I needed any booze. I'll show that cheap drummer I don't have to have any Dutch courage—

Guiltily.

But he's been very kind and generous staking me. He can't help his insulting manner, I suppose.

He turns away from the bar.

My legs are a bit shaky yet. I better sit down a while.

He goes back and sits at the left of the second table, facing PARRITT, *who gives him a scowling, suspicious glance and then ignores him.* ROCKY *looks at* CHUCK *and taps his head disgustedly.* CAPTAIN LEWIS *appears in the doorway from the hall.*

CHUCK

Mutters.

Here's anudder one.

LEWIS *looks spruce and clean-shaven. His ancient tweed suit has been brushed and his frayed linen is clean. His manner is full of a forced, jaunty self-assurance. But he is sick and beset by katzenjammer.*

LEWIS

Good morning, gentlemen all.

He passes along the front of bar to look out in the street.

A jolly fine morning, too.

He turns back to the bar.

An eye-opener? I think not. Not required, Rocky, old chum. Feel extremely fit, as a matter of fact. Though can't say I slept much, thanks to that interfering ass, Hickey, and that stupid bounder of a Boer.

His face hardens.

I've had about all I can take from that fellow. It's my own fault, of course, for allowing a brute of a Dutch farmer to become familiar. Well, it's come to a parting of the ways now, and good riddance. Which reminds me, here's my key.

He puts it on the bar.

I shan't be coming back. Sorry to be leaving good old Harry and the rest of you, of course, but I can't continue to live under the same roof with that fellow.

He stops, stiffening into hostility as WETJOEN *enters from the hall, and pointedly turns his back on him.* WETJOEN *glares at him sneeringly. He, too, has made an effort to spruce up his appearance, and his bearing has a forced swagger of conscious physical strength. Behind this, he is sick and feebly holding his booze-sodden body together.*

ROCKY

To LEWIS—*disgustedly putting the key on the shelf in back of the bar.*

So Hickey's kidded the pants offa you, too? Yuh tink yuh're leavin' here, huh?

WETJOEN

Jeeringly.

Ja! Dot's vhat he kids himself.

LEWIS

Ignores him—airily.

Yes, I'm leaving, Rocky. But that ass, Hickey, has nothing to do with it. Been thinking things over. Time I turned over a new leaf, and all that.

WETJOEN
He's going to get a job! Dot's what he says!

ROCKY
What at, for Chris' sake?

LEWIS
Keeping his airy manner.
Oh, anything. I mean, not manual labor, naturally, but anything that calls for a bit of brains and education. However humble. Beggars can't be choosers. I'll see a pal of mine at the Consulate. He promised any time I felt an energetic fit he'd get me a post with the Cunard—clark in the office or something of the kind.

WETJOEN
Ja! At Limey Consulate they promise anything to get rid of him when he comes there tronk! They're scared to call the police and have him pinched because it vould scandal in the papers make about a Limey officer and chentleman!

LEWIS
As a matter of fact, Rocky, I only wish a post temporarily. Means to an end, you know. Save up enough for a first-class passage home, that's the bright idea.

WETJOEN
He's sailing back to home, sveet home! Dot's biggest pipe dream of all. What leetle brain the poor Limey has left, dot isn't in whiskey pickled, Hickey has made crazy!
LEWIS' *fists clench, but he manages to ignore this.*

CHUCK
Feels sorry for LEWIS *and turns on* WETJOEN—*sarcastically.*
Hickey ain't made no sucker outa you, huh? You're too foxy, huh? But I'll bet you tink yuh're goin' out and land a job, too.

WETJOEN
Bristles.
I am, ja. For me, it is easy. Because I put on no airs of chentleman.

I am not ashamed to vork vith my hands. I vas a farmer before the war ven ploody Limey thieves steal my country.

Boastfully.

Anyone I ask for job can see vith one look I have the great strength to do work of ten ordinary mens.

LEWIS

Sneeringly.

Yes, Chuck, you remember he gave a demonstration of his extraordinary muscles last night when he helped to move the piano.

CHUCK

Yuh couldn't even hold up your corner. It was your fault de damned box almost fell down de stairs.

WETJOEN

My hands vas sweaty! Could I help dot my hands slip? I could de whole veight of it lift! In old days in Transvaal, I lift loaded oxcart by the axle! So vhy shouldn't I get job? Dot longshoreman boss, Dan, he tell me any time I like, he take me on. And Benny from de Market he promise me same.

LEWIS

You remember, Rocky, it was one of those rare occasions when the Boer that walks like a man — spelled with a double o, by the way — was buying drinks and Dan and Benny were stony. They'd bloody well have promised him the moon.

ROCKY

Yeah, yuh big boob, dem boids was on'y kiddin' yuh.

WETJOEN

Angrily.

Dot's lie! You vill see dis morning I get job! I'll show dot bloody Limey chentleman, and dot liar, Hickey! And I need vork only leetle vhile to save money for my passage home. I need not much money because I am not ashamed to travel steerage. I don't put on first-cabin airs!

Tauntingly.

Und *I can* go home to my country! Vhen I get there, they vill let *me* come in!

LEWIS
Grows rigid—his voice trembling with repressed anger.
There was a rumor in South Africa, Rocky, that a certain Boer officer—if you call the leaders of a rabble of farmers officers—kept advising Cronje to retreat and not stand and fight—

WETJOEN
And I vas right! I vas right! He got surrounded at Poardeberg! He had to surrender!

LEWIS
Ignoring him.
Good strategy, no doubt, but a suspicion grew afterwards into a conviction among the Boers that the officer's caution was prompted by a desire to make his personal escape. His countrymen felt extremely savage about it, and his family disowned him. So I imagine there would be no welcoming committee waiting on the dock, nor delighted relatives making the veldt ring with their happy cries—

WETJOEN
With guilty rage.
All lies! You Gottamned Limey—
Trying to control himself and copy LEWIS' *manner.*
I also haf heard rumors of a Limey officer who, after the war, lost all his money gambling vhen he vas tronk. But they found out it vas regiment money, too, he lost—

LEWIS
Loses his control and starts for him.
You bloody Dutch scum!

ROCKY
Leans over the bar and stops LEWIS *with a straight-arm swipe on the chest.*
Cut it out!
At the same moment CHUCK *grabs* WETJOEN *and yanks him back.*

WETJOEN

Struggling.

Let him come! I saw them come before—at Modder River, Magers-fontein, Spion Kopje—waving their silly swords, so afraid they couldn't show off how brave they vas!—and I kill them vith my rifle so easy!

Vindictively.

Listen to me, you Cecil! Often when I am tronk and kidding you I say I am sorry I missed you, but now, py Gott, I am sober, and I don't joke, and I say it!

LARRY

Gives a sardonic guffaw—with his comically crazy, intense whisper.

Be God, you can't say Hickey hasn't the miraculous touch to raise the dead, when he can start the Boer War raging again!

This interruption acts like a cold douche on LEWIS *and* WETJOEN. *They subside, and* ROCKY *and* CHUCK *let go of them.* LEWIS *turns his back on the Boer.*

LEWIS

Attempting a return to his jaunty manner, as if nothing had happened.

Well, time I was on my merry way to see my chap at the Consulate. The early bird catches the job, what? Good-bye and good luck, Rocky, and everyone.

He starts for the street door.

WETJOEN

Py Gott, if dot Limey can go, I can go!

He hurries after LEWIS. *But* LEWIS, *his hand about to push the swinging doors open, hesitates, as though struck by a sudden paralysis of the will, and* WETJOEN *has to jerk back to avoid bumping into him. For a second they stand there, one behind the other, staring over the swinging doors into the street.*

ROCKY

Well, why don't yuh beat it?

LEWIS

Guiltily casual.

Eh? Oh, just happened to think. Hardly the decent thing to pop off without saying good-bye to old Harry. One of the best, Harry. And good old Jimmy, too. They ought to be down any moment.

He pretends to notice WETJOEN *for the first time and steps away from the door—apologizing as to a stranger.*

Sorry. I seem to be blocking your way out.

WETJOEN

Stiffly.

No. I vait to say good-bye to Harry and Jimmy, too.

He goes to right of door behind the lunch counter and looks through the window, his back to the room. LEWIS *takes up a similar stand at the window on the left of door.*

CHUCK

Jees, can yuh beat dem simps!

He picks up CORA's *drink at the end of the bar.*

Hell, I'd forgot Cora. She'll be trowin' a fit.

He goes into the hall with the drink.

ROCKY

Looks after him disgustedly.

Dat's right, wait on her and spoil her, yuh poor sap!

He shakes his head and begins to wipe the bar mechanically.

WILLIE

Is regarding PARRITT *across the table from him with an eager, calculating eye. He leans over and speaks in a low confidential tone.*

Look here, Parritt. I'd like to have a talk with you.

PARRITT

Starts—scowling defensively.

What about?

WILLIE

His manner becoming his idea of a crafty criminal lawyer's.

About the trouble you're in. Oh, I know. You don't admit it. You're quite right. That's my advice. Deny everything. Keep your mouth shut. Make no statements whatever without first consulting your attorney.

PARRITT
Say! What the hell—?

WILLIE
But you can trust me. I'm a lawyer, and it's just occurred to me you and I ought to co-operate. Of course I'm going to see the D.A. this morning about a job on his staff. But that may take time. There may not be an immediate opening. Meanwhile it would be a good idea for me to take a case or two, on my own, and prove my brilliant record in law school was no flash in the pan. So why not retain me as your attorney?

PARRITT
You're crazy! What do I want with a lawyer?

WILLIE
That's right. Don't admit anything. But you can trust me, so let's not beat about the bush. You got in trouble out on the Coast, eh? And now you're hiding out. Any fool can spot that.
Lowering his voice still more.
You feel safe here, and maybe you are, for a while. But remember, they get you in the end. I know from my father's experience. No one could have felt safer than he did. When anyone mentioned the law to him, he nearly died laughing. But—

PARRITT
You crazy mutt!
Turning to LARRY *with a strained laugh.*
Did you get that, Larry? This damned fool thinks the cops are after me!

LARRY
Bursts out with his true reaction before he thinks to ignore him.
I wish to God they were! And so should you, if you had the honor of a louse!
PARRITT *stares into his eyes guiltily for a second. Then he smiles sneeringly.*

PARRITT

And you're the guy who kids himself he's through with the Movement! You old lying faker, you're still in love with it!

LARRY *ignores him again now.*

WILLIE

Disappointedly.

Then you're not in trouble, Parritt? I was hoping— But never mind. No offense meant. Forget it.

PARRITT

Condescendingly—his eyes on LARRY.

Sure. That's all right, Willie. I'm not sore at you. It's that damned old faker that gets my goat.

He slips out of his chair and goes quietly over to sit in the chair beside LARRY *he had occupied before—in a low, insinuating, intimate tone.*

I think I understand, Larry. It's really Mother you still love—isn't it?—in spite of the dirty deal she gave you. But hell, what did you expect? She was never true to anyone but herself and the Movement. But I understand how you can't help still feeling—because I still love her, too.

Pleading in a strained, desperate tone.

You know I do, don't you? You must! So you see I couldn't have expected they'd catch her! You've got to believe me that I sold them out just to get a few lousy dollars to blow in on a whore. No other reason, honest! There couldn't possibly be any other reason!

Again he has a strange air of exonerating himself from guilt by this shameless confession.

LARRY

Trying not to listen, has listened with increasing tension.

For the love of Christ will you leave me in peace! I've told you you can't make me judge you! But if you don't keep still, you'll be saying something soon that will make you vomit your own soul like a drink of nickel rotgut that won't stay down!

He pushes back his chair and springs to his feet.

To hell with you!

He goes to the bar.

PARRITT

Jumps up and starts to follow him—desperately.

Don't go, Larry! You've got to help me!

But LARRY *is at the bar, back turned, and* ROCKY *is scowling at him. He stops, shrinking back into himself helplessly, and turns away. He goes to the table where he had been before, and this time he takes the chair at rear facing directly front. He puts his elbows on the table, holding his head in his hands as if he had a splitting headache.*

LARRY

Set 'em up, Rocky. I swore I'd have no more drinks on Hickey, if I died of drought, but I've changed my mind! Be God, he owes it to me, and I'd get blind to the world now if it was the Iceman of Death himself treating!

He stops, startledly, a superstitious awe coming into his face.

What made me say that, I wonder.

With a sardonic laugh.

Well, be God, it fits, for Death was the Iceman Hickey called to his home!

ROCKY

Aw, forget dat iceman gag! De poor dame is dead.

Pushing a bottle and glass at LARRY.

Gwan and get paralyzed! I'll be glad to see one bum in dis dump act natural.

LARRY *downs a drink and pours another.*

ED MOSHER *appears in the doorway from the hall. The same change which is apparent in the manner and appearance of the others shows in him. He is sick, his nerves are shattered, his eyes are apprehensive, but he, too, puts on an exaggeratedly self-confident bearing. He saunters to the bar between* LARRY *and the street entrance.*

MOSHER

Morning, Rocky. Hello, Larry. Glad to see Brother Hickey hasn't corrupted you to temperance. I wouldn't mind a shot myself.

As ROCKY *shoves a bottle toward him he shakes his head.*

But I remember the only breath-killer in this dump is coffee beans.

The boss would never fall for that. No man can run a circus successfully who believes guys chew coffee beans because they like them.

He pushes the bottle away.

No, much as I need one after the hell of a night I've had—

He scowls.

That drummer son of a drummer! I had to lock him out. But I could hear him through the wall doing his spiel to someone all night long. Still at it with Jimmy and Harry when I came down just now. But the hardest to take was that flannel-mouth, flatfoot Mick trying to tell me where I got off! I had to lock him out, too.

As he says this, MCGLOIN *comes in the doorway from the hall. The change in his appearance and manner is identical with that of* MOSHER *and the others.*

MCGLOIN

He's a liar, Rocky! It was me locked him out!

MOSHER *starts to flare up—then ignores him. They turn their backs on each other.* MCGLOIN *starts into the back-room section.*

WILLIE

Come and sit here, Mac. You're just the man I want to see. If I'm to take your case, we ought to have a talk before we leave.

MCGLOIN

Contemptuously.

We'll have no talk. You damned fool, do you think I'd have your father's son for my lawyer? They'd take one look at you and bounce us both out on our necks!

WILLIE *winces and shrinks down in his chair.* MCGLOIN *goes to the first table beyond him and sits with his back to the bar.*

I don't need a lawyer, anyway. To hell with the law! All I've got to do is see the right ones and get them to pass the word. They will, too. They know I was framed. And once they've passed the word, it's as good as done, law or no law.

MOSHER

God, I'm glad I'm leaving this madhouse!

He pulls his key from his pocket and slaps it on the bar.

Here's my key, Rocky.

MCGLOIN

Pulls his from his pocket.

And here's mine.

He tosses it to ROCKY.

I'd rather sleep in the gutter than pass another night under the same roof with that loon, Hickey, and a lying circus grifter!

He adds darkly.

And if that hat fits anyone here, let him put it on!

MOSHER *turns toward him furiously but* ROCKY *leans over the bar and grabs his arm.*

ROCKY

Nix! Take it easy!

MOSHER *subsides.* ROCKY *tosses the keys on the shelf—disgustedly.*

You boids gimme a pain. It'd soive you right if I wouldn't give de keys back to yuh tonight.

They both turn on him resentfully, but there is an interruption as CORA *appears in the doorway from the hall with* CHUCK *behind her. She is drunk, dressed in her gaudy best, her face plastered with rouge and mascara, her hair a bit disheveled, her hat on anyhow.*

CORA

Comes a few steps inside the bar—with a strained bright giggle.

Hello, everybody! Here we go! Hickey just told us, ain't it time we beat it, if we're really goin'. So we're showin' de bastard, ain't we, Honey? He's comin' right down wid Harry and Jimmy. Jees, dem two look like dey was goin' to de electric chair!

With frightened anger.

If I had to listen to any more of Hickey's bunk, I'd brain him.

She puts her hand on CHUCK's *arm.*

Come on, Honey. Let's get started before he comes down.

CHUCK

Sullenly.

Sure, anyting yuh say, Baby.

CORA

Turns on him truculently.

Yeah? Well, I say we stop at de foist reg'lar dump and yuh gotta blow me to a sherry flip—or four or five, if I want 'em!—or all bets is off!

CHUCK

Aw, yuh got a fine bun on now!

CORA

Cheap skate! I know what's eatin' you, Tightwad! Well, use my dough, den, if yuh're so stingy. Yuh'll grab it all, anyway, right after de ceremony. I know you!
She hikes her skirt up and reaches inside the top of her stocking.
Here, yuh big tramp!

CHUCK

Knocks her hand away—angrily.
Keep your lousy dough! And don't show off your legs to dese bums when yuh're goin' to be married, if yuh don't want a sock in de puss!

CORA

Pleased—meekly.
Aw right, Honey.
Looking around with a foolish laugh.
Say, why don't all you barflies come to de weddin'?
But they are all sunk in their own apprehensions and ignore her. She hesitates, miserably uncertain.
Well, we're goin', guys.
There is no comment. Her eyes fasten on ROCKY—*desperately.*
Say, Rocky, yuh gone deef? I said me and Chuck was goin' now.

ROCKY

Wiping the bar—with elaborate indifference.
Well, good-bye. Give my love to Joisey.

CORA

Tearfully indignant.
Ain't yuh goin' to wish us happiness, yuh doity little Ginny?

ROCKY

Sure. Here's hopin' yuh don't moider each odder before next week.

CHUCK

Angrily.

Aw, Baby, what d'we care for dat pimp?

ROCKY *turns on him threateningly, but* CHUCK *hears someone upstairs in the hall and grabs* CORA's *arm.*

Here's Hickey comin'! Let's get outa here!

They hurry into the hall. The street door is heard slamming behind them.

ROCKY

Gloomily pronounces an obituary.

One regular guy and one all-right tart gone to hell!

Fiercely.

Dat louse Hickey oughta be croaked!

There is a muttered growl of assent from most of the gathering. Then HARRY HOPE *enters from the hall, followed by* JIMMY TOMORROW, *with* HICKEY *on his heels.* HOPE *and* JIMMY *are both putting up a front of self-assurance, but* CORA's *description of them was apt. There is a desperate bluff in their manner as they walk in, which suggests the last march of the condemned.* HOPE *is dressed in an old black Sunday suit, black tie, shoes, socks, which give him the appearance of being in mourning.* JIMMY's *clothes are pressed, his shoes shined, his white linen immaculate. He has a hangover and his gently appealing dog's eyes have a boiled look.* HICKEY's *face is a bit drawn from lack of sleep and his voice is hoarse from continual talking, but his bustling energy appears nervously intensified, and his beaming expression is one of triumphant accomplishment.*

HICKEY

Well, here we are! We've got this far, at least!

He pats JIMMY *on the back.*

Good work, Jimmy. I told you you weren't half as sick as you pretended. No excuse whatever for postponing—

JIMMY

I'll thank you to keep your hands off me! I merely mentioned I would feel more fit tomorrow. But it might as well be today, I suppose.

HICKEY

Finish it now, so it'll be dead forever, and you can be free!

He passes him to clap HOPE *encouragingly on the shoulder.*

Cheer up, Harry. You found your rheumatism didn't bother you coming downstairs, didn't you? I told you it wouldn't.

He winks around at the others. With the exception of HUGO *and* PARRITT, *all their eyes are fixed on him with bitter animosity. He gives* HOPE *a playful nudge in the ribs.*

You're the damnedest one for alibis, Governor! As bad as Jimmy!

HOPE

Putting on his deaf manner.

Eh? I can't hear—

Defiantly.

You're a liar! I've had rheumatism on and off for twenty years. Ever since Bessie died. Everybody knows that.

HICKEY

Yes, we know it's the kind of rheumatism you turn on and off! We're on to you, you old faker!

He claps him on the shoulder again, chuckling.

HOPE

Looks humiliated and guilty—by way of escape he glares around at the others.

Bejees, what are all you bums hanging round staring at me for? Think you was watching a circus! Why don't you get the hell out of here and 'tend to your own business, like Hickey's told you?

They look at him reproachfully, their eyes hurt. They fidget as if trying to move.

HICKEY

Yes, Harry, I certainly thought they'd have had the guts to be gone by this time.

He grins.

Or maybe I did have my doubts.

Abruptly he becomes sincerely sympathetic and earnest.

Because I know exactly what you're up against, boys. I know how damned yellow a man can be when it comes to making himself face the truth. I've been through the mill, and I had to face a worse bastard in myself than any of you will have to in yourselves. I know you become such a coward you'll grab at any lousy excuse to get out of killing your pipe dreams. And yet, as I've told you over and over, it's exactly those damned tomorrow dreams which keep you from making peace with yourself. So you've got to kill them like I did mine.

He pauses. They glare at him with fear and hatred. They seem about to curse him, to spring at him. But they remain silent and motionless. His manner changes and he becomes kindly bullying.

Come on, boys! Get moving! Who'll start the ball rolling? You, Captain, and you, General. You're nearest the door. And besides, you're old war heroes! You ought to lead the forlorn hope! Come on, now, show us a little of that good old battle of Modder River spirit we've heard so much about! You can't hang around all day looking as if you were scared the street outside would bite you!

LEWIS
Turns with humiliated rage—with an attempt at jaunty casualness.
Right you are, Mister Bloody Nosey Parker! Time I pushed off. Was only waiting to say good-bye to you, Harry, old chum.

HOPE
Dejectedly.
Good-bye, Captain. Hope you have luck.

LEWIS
Oh, I'm bound to, Old Chap, and the same to you.
He pushes the swinging doors open and makes a brave exit, turning to his right and marching off outside the window at right of door.

WETJOEN
Py Gott, if dot Limey can, I can!
He pushes the door open and lumbers through it like a bull charging an obstacle. He turns left and disappears off rear, outside the farthest window.

HICKEY
Exhortingly.

Next? Come on, Ed. It's a fine summer's day and the call of the old circus lot must be in your blood!

MOSHER *glares at him, then goes to the door.* MCGLOIN *jumps up from his chair and starts moving toward the door.* HICKEY *claps him on the back as he passes.*

That's the stuff, Mac.

MOSHER
Good-bye, Harry.
He goes out, turning right outside.

MCGLOIN
Glowering after him.
If that crooked grifter has the guts—
He goes out, turning left outside. HICKEY *glances at* WILLIE *who, before he can speak, jumps from his chair.*

WILLIE
Good-bye, Harry, and thanks for all your kindness.

HICKEY
Claps him on the back.
That's the way, Willie! The D.A.'s a busy man. He can't wait all day for you, you know.
WILLIE *hurries to the door.*

HOPE
Dully.
Good luck, Willie.
WILLIE *goes out and turns right outside. While he is doing so,* JIMMY, *in a sick panic, sneaks to the bar and furtively reaches for* LARRY'S *glass of whiskey.*

HICKEY
And now it's your turn, Jimmy, old pal.
He sees what JIMMY *is at and grabs his arm just as he is about to down the drink.*
Now, now, Jimmy! You can't do that to yourself. One drink on top of your hangover and an empty stomach and you'll be oreyeyed.

Then you'll tell yourself you wouldn't stand a chance if you went up soused to get your old job back.

JIMMY
Pleads abjectly.
Tomorrow! I will tomorrow! I'll be in good shape tomorrow!
Abruptly getting control of himself—with shaken firmness.
All right. I'm going. Take your hands off me.

HICKEY
That's the ticket! You'll thank me when it's all over.

JIMMY
In a burst of futile fury.
You dirty swine!
He tries to throw the drink in HICKEY's *face, but his aim is poor and it lands on* HICKEY's *coat.* JIMMY *turns and dashes through the door, disappearing outside the window at right of door.*

HICKEY
Brushing the whiskey off his coat—humorously.
All set for an alcohol rub! But no hard feelings. I know how he feels. I wrote the book. I've seen the day when if anyone forced me to face the truth about my pipe dreams, I'd have shot them dead.
He turns to HOPE—*encouragingly.*
Well, Governor, Jimmy made the grade. It's up to you. If he's got the guts to go through with the test, then certainly you—

LARRY
Bursts out.
Leave Harry alone, damn you!

HICKEY
Grins at him.
I'd make up my mind about myself if I was you, Larry, and not bother over Harry. He'll come through all right. I've promised him that. He doesn't need anyone's bum pity. Do you, Governor?

HOPE
With a pathetic attempt at his old fuming assertiveness.

No, bejees! Keep your nose out of this, Larry. What's Hickey got to do with it? I've always been going to take this walk, ain't I? Bejees, you bums want to keep me locked up in here 's if I was in jail! I've stood it long enough! I'm free, white and twenty-one, and I'll do as I damned please, bejees! You keep your nose out, too, Hickey! You'd think you was boss of this dump, not me. Sure, I'm all right! Why shouldn't I be? What the hell's to be scared of, just taking a stroll around my own ward?

As he talks he has been moving toward the door. Now he reaches it.
What's the weather like outside, Rocky?

ROCKY
Fine day, Boss.

HOPE
What's that? Can't hear you. Don't look fine to me. Looks 's if it'd pour down cats and dogs any minute. My rheumatism—
He catches himself.
No, must be my eyes. Half blind, bejees. Makes things look black. I see now it's a fine day. Too damned hot for a walk, though, if you ask me. Well, do me good to sweat the booze out of me. But I'll have to watch out for the damned automobiles. Wasn't none of them around the last time, twenty years ago. From what I've seen of 'em through the window, they'd run over you as soon as look at you. Not that I'm scared of 'em. I can take care of myself.
He puts a reluctant hand on the swinging door.
Well, so long—
He stops and looks back—with frightened irascibility.
Bejees, where are you, Hickey? It's time we got started.

HICKEY
Grins and shakes his head.
No, Harry. Can't be done. You've got to keep a date with yourself alone.

HOPE
With forced fuming.
Hell of a guy, you are! Thought you'd be willing to help me across the street, knowing I'm half blind. Half deaf, too. Can't bear those

damned automobiles. Hell with you! Bejees, I've never needed no one's help and I don't now!

Egging himself on.

I'll take a good long walk now I've started. See all my old friends. Bejees, they must have given me up for dead. Twenty years is a long time. But they know it was grief over Bessie's death that made me—

He puts his hand on the door.

Well, the sooner I get started—

Then he drops his hand—with sentimental melancholy.

You know, Hickey, that's what gets me. Can't help thinking the last time I went out was to Bessie's funeral. After she'd gone, I didn't feel life was worth living. Swore I'd never go out again.

Pathetically.

Somehow, I can't feel it's right for me to go, Hickey, even now. It's like I was doing wrong to her memory.

HICKEY

Now, Governor, you can't let yourself get away with that one any more!

HOPE

Cupping his hand to his ear.

What's that? Can't hear you.

Sentimentally again but with desperation.

I remember now clear as day the last time before she— It was a fine Sunday morning. We went out to church together.

His voice breaks on a sob.

HICKEY

Amused.

It's a great act, Governor. But I know better, and so do you. You never did want to go to church or any place else with her. She was always on your neck, making you have ambition and go out and do things, when all you wanted was to get drunk in peace.

HOPE

Falteringly.

Can't hear a word you're saying. You're a God-damned liar, anyway!

Then in a sudden fury, his voice trembling with hatred.

Bejees, you son of a bitch, if there was a mad dog outside I'd go and shake hands with it rather than stay here with you!

The momentum of his fit of rage does it. He pushes the door open and strides blindly out into the street and as blindly past the window behind the free-lunch counter.

ROCKY

In amazement.

Jees, he made it! I'd a give yuh fifty to one he'd never—

He goes to the end of the bar to look through the window—disgustedly.

Aw, he's stopped. I'll bet yuh he's comin' back.

HICKEY

Of course, he's coming back. So are all the others. By tonight they'll all be here again. You dumbbell, that's the whole point.

ROCKY

Excitedly.

No, he ain't either! He's gone to de coib. He's lookin' up and down. Scared stiff of automobiles. Jees, dey ain't more'n two an hour comes down dis street, de old boob!

He watches excitedly, as if it were a race he had a bet on, oblivious to what happens in the bar.

LARRY

Turns on HICKEY *with bitter defiance.*

And now it's my turn, I suppose? What is it I'm to do to achieve this blessed peace of yours?

HICKEY

Grins at him.

Why, we've discussed all that, Larry. Just stop lying to yourself—

LARRY

You think when I say I'm finished with life, and tired of watching the stupid greed of the human circus, and I'll welcome closing my eyes in the long sleep of death—you think that's a coward's lie?

HICKEY

Chuckling.

Well, what do you think, Larry?

LARRY

With increasing bitter intensity, more as if he were fighting with himself than with HICKEY.

I'm afraid to live, am I?—and even more afraid to die! So I sit here, with my pride drowned on the bottom of a bottle, keeping drunk so I won't see myself shaking in my britches with fright, or hear myself whining and praying: Beloved Christ, let me live a little longer at any price! If it's only for a few days more, or a few hours even, have mercy, Almighty God, and let me still clutch greedily to my yellow heart this sweet treasure, this jewel beyond price, the dirty, stinking bit of withered old flesh which is my beautiful little life!

He laughs with a sneering, vindictive self-loathing, staring inward at himself with contempt and hatred. Then abruptly he makes HICKEY *again the antagonist.*

You think you'll make me admit that to myself?

HICKEY

Chuckling.

But you just did admit it, didn't you?

PARRITT

Lifts his head from his hands to glare at LARRY—*jeeringly.*

That's the stuff, Hickey! Show the old yellow faker up! He can't play dead on me like this! He's got to help me!

HICKEY

Yes, Larry, you've got to settle with him. I'm leaving you entirely in his hands. He'll do as good a job as I could at making you give up that old grandstand bluff.

LARRY

Angrily.

I'll see the two of you in hell first!

ROCKY

Calls excitedly from the end of the bar.

Jees, Harry's startin' across de street! He's goin' to fool yuh, Hickey, yuh bastard!

He pauses, watching—then worriedly.

What de hell's he stoppin' for? Right in de middle of de street! Yuh'd
tink he was paralyzed or somethin'!
Disgustedly.
Aw, he's quittin'! He's turned back! Jees, look at de old bastard travel!
Here he comes!
*Hope passes the window outside the free-lunch counter in a shambling,
panic-stricken run. He comes lurching blindly through the swinging
doors and stumbles to the bar at LARRY's right.*

HOPE

Bejees, give me a drink quick! Scared me out of a year's growth!
Bejees, that guy ought to be pinched! Bejees, it ain't safe to walk in
the streets! Bejees, that ends me! Never again! Give me that bottle!
*He slops a glass full and drains it and pours another— To ROCKY, who
is regarding him with scorn—appealingly.*
You seen it, didn't you, Rocky?

ROCKY
Seen what?

HOPE

That automobile, you dumb Wop! Feller driving it must be drunk
or crazy. He'd run right over me if I hadn't jumped.
Ingratiatingly.
Come on, Larry, have a drink. Everybody have a drink. Have a cigar,
Rocky. I know you hardly ever touch it.

ROCKY
Resentfully.
Well, dis is de time I do touch it!
Pouring a drink.
I'm goin' to get stinko, see! And if yuh don't like it, yuh know what
yuh can do! I gotta good mind to chuck my job, anyways.
Disgustedly.
Jees, Harry, I thought yuh had some guts! I was bettin' yuh'd make
it and show dat four-flusher up.
He nods at HICKEY—then snorts.
Automobile, hell! Who d'yuh tink yuh're kiddin'? Dey wasn' no
automobile! Yuh just quit cold!

HOPE

Feebly.

Guess I ought to know! Bejees, it almost killed me!

HICKEY

Comes to the bar between him and LARRY, *and puts a hand on his shoulder—kindly.*

Now, now, Governor. Don't be foolish. You've faced the test and come through. You're rid of all that nagging dream stuff now. You know you can't believe it any more.

HOPE

Appeals pleadingly to LARRY.

Larry, you saw it, didn't you? Drink up! Have another! Have all you want! Bejees, we'll go on a grand old souse together! You saw that automobile, didn't you?

LARRY

Compassionately, avoiding his eyes.

Sure, I saw it, Harry. You had a narrow escape. Be God, I thought you were a goner!

HICKEY

Turns on him with a flash of sincere indignation.

What the hell's the matter with you, Larry? You know what I told you about the wrong kind of pity. Leave Harry alone! You'd think I was trying to harm him, the fool way you act! My oldest friend! What kind of a louse do you think I am? There isn't anything I wouldn't do for Harry, and he knows it! All I've wanted to do is fix it so he'll be finally at peace with himself for the rest of his days! And if you'll only wait until the final returns are in, you'll find that's exactly what I've accomplished!

He turns to HOPE *and pats his shoulder—coaxingly.*

Come now, Governor. What's the use of being stubborn, now when it's all over and dead? Give up that ghost automobile.

HOPE

Beginning to collapse within himself—dully.

Yes, what's the use—now? All a lie! No automobile. But, bejees, something ran over me! Must have been myself, I guess.

He forces a feeble smile—then wearily.

Guess I'll sit down. Feel all in. Like a corpse, bejees.

He picks a bottle and glass from the bar and walks to the first table and slumps down in the chair, facing left-front. His shaking hand misjudges the distance and he sets the bottle on the table with a jar that rouses HUGO, *who lifts his head from his arms and blinks at him through his thick spectacles.* HOPE *speaks to him in a flat, dead voice.*

Hello, Hugo. Coming up for air? Stay passed out, that's the right dope. There ain't any cool willow trees—except you grow your own in a bottle.

He pours a drink and gulps it down.

HUGO

With his silly giggle.

Hello, Harry, stupid proletarian monkey-face! I vill trink champagne beneath the villow—

With a change to aristocratic fastidiousness.

But the slaves must ice it properly!

With guttural rage.

Gottamned Hickey! Peddler pimp for nouveau-riche capitalism! Vhen I lead the jackass mob to the sack of Babylon, I vill make them hang him to a lamppost the first one!

HOPE

Spiritlessly.

Good work. I'll help pull on the rope. Have a drink, Hugo.

HUGO

Frightenedly.

No, thank you. I am too trunk now. I hear myself say crazy things. Do not listen, please. Larry vill tell you I haf never been so crazy trunk. I must sleep it off.

He starts to put his head on his arms but stops and stares at HOPE *with growing uneasiness.*

Vhat's matter, Harry? You look funny. You look dead. Vhat's happened? I don't know you. Listen, I feel I am dying, too. Because I am so crazy trunk! It is very necessary I sleep. But I can't sleep here vith you. You look dead.

He scrambles to his feet in a confused panic, turns his back on HOPE *and settles into the chair at the next table which faces left. He thrusts his head down on his arms like an ostrich hiding its head in the sand. He does not notice* PARRITT, *nor* PARRITT *him.*

LARRY
To HICKEY *with bitter condemnation.*
Another one who's begun to enjoy your peace!

HICKEY
Oh, I know it's tough on him right now, the same as it is on Harry. But that's only the first shock. I promise you they'll both come through all right.

LARRY
And you believe that! I see you do! You mad fool!

HICKEY
Of course, I believe it! I tell you I know from my own experience!

HOPE
Spiritlessly.
Close that big clam of yours, Hickey. Bejees, you're a worse gabber than that nagging bitch, Bessie, was.
He drinks his drink mechanically and pours another.

ROCKY
In amazement.
Jees, did yuh hear dat?

HOPE
Dully.
What's wrong with this booze? There's no kick in it.

ROCKY
Worriedly.
Jees, Larry, Hugo had it right. He does look like he'd croaked.

HICKEY

Annoyed.

Don't be a damned fool! Give him time. He's coming along all right.
He calls to HOPE *with a first trace of underlying uneasiness.*
You're all right, aren't you, Harry?

HOPE

Dully.

I want to pass out like Hugo.

LARRY

Turns to HICKEY—*with bitter anger.*
It's the peace of death you've brought him.

HICKEY

For the first time loses his temper.

That's a lie!

But he controls this instantly and grins.

Well, well, you did manage to get a rise out of me that time. I think
such a hell of a lot of Harry—
Impatiently.

You know that's damned foolishness. Look at me. I've been through
it. Do I look dead? Just leave Harry alone and wait until the shock
wears off and you'll see. He'll be a new man. Like I am.
He called to HOPE *coaxingly.*

How's it coming, Governor? Beginning to feel free, aren't you? Relieved and not guilty any more?

HOPE

Grumbles spiritlessly.

Bejees, you must have been monkeying with the booze, too, you
interfering bastard! There's no life in it now. I want to get drunk and
pass out. Let's all pass out. Who the hell cares?

HICKEY

Lowering his voice—worriedly to LARRY.

I admit I didn't think he'd be hit so hard. He's always been a happy-
go-lucky slob. Like I was. Of course, it hit me hard, too. But only
for a minute. Then I felt as if a ton of guilt had been lifted off my

mind. I saw what had happened was the only possible way for the peace of all concerned.

LARRY
Sharply.
What was it happened? Tell us that! And don't try to get out of it! I want a straight answer!
Vindictively.
I think it was something you drove someone else to do!

HICKEY
Puzzled.
Someone else?

LARRY
Accusingly.
What did your wife die of? You've kept that a deep secret, I notice — for some reason!

HICKEY
Reproachfully.
You're not very considerate, Larry. But, if you insist on knowing now, there's no reason you shouldn't. It was a bullet through the head that killed Evelyn.
There is a second's tense silence.

HOPE
Dully.
Who the hell cares? To hell with her and that nagging old hag, Bessie.

ROCKY
Christ. You had de right dope, Larry.

LARRY
Revengefully.
You drove your poor wife to suicide? I knew it! Be God, I don't blame her! I'd almost do as much myself to be rid of you! It's what you'd like to drive us all to —
Abruptly he is ashamed of himself and pitying.
I'm sorry, Hickey. I'm a rotten louse to throw that in your face.

HICKEY

Quietly.

Oh, that's all right, Larry. But don't jump at conclusions. I didn't say poor Evelyn committed suicide. It's the last thing she'd ever have done, as long as I was alive for her to take care of and forgive. If you'd known her at all, you'd never get such a crazy suspicion.

He pauses — then slowly.

No, I'm sorry to have to tell you my poor wife was killed.

LARRY *stares at him with growing horror and shrinks back along the bar away from him.* PARRITT *jerks his head up from his hands and looks around frightenedly, not at* HICKEY, *but at* LARRY. ROCKY's *round eyes are popping.* HOPE *stares dully at the table top.* HUGO, *his head hidden in his arms, gives no sign of life.*

LARRY

Shakenly.

Then she — was murdered.

PARRITT

Springs to his feet — stammers defensively.

You're a liar, Larry! You must be crazy to say that to me! You know she's still alive!

But no one pays any attention to him.

ROCKY

Blurts out.

Moidered? Who done it?

LARRY

His eyes fixed with fascinated horror on HICKEY — *frightenedly.*

Don't ask questions, you dumb Wop! It's none of our damned business! Leave Hickey alone!

HICKEY

Smiles at him with affectionate amusement.

Still the old grandstand bluff, Larry? Or is it some more bum pity?

He turns to ROCKY — *matter-of-factly.*

The police don't know who killed her yet, Rocky. But I expect they will before very long.

As if that finished the subject, he comes forward to HOPE *and sits beside him, with an arm around his shoulder—affectionately coaxing.*

Coming along fine now, aren't you, Governor? Getting over the first shock? Beginning to feel free from guilt and lying hopes and at peace with yourself?

HOPE

With a dull callousness.

Somebody croaked your Evelyn, eh? Bejees, my bets are on the iceman! But who the hell cares? Let's get drunk and pass out.

He tosses down his drink with a lifeless, automatic movement—complainingly.

Bejees, what did you do to the booze, Hickey? There's no damned life left in it.

PARRITT

Stammers, his eyes on LARRY, *whose eyes in turn remain fixed on* HICKEY.

Don't look like that, Larry! You've got to believe what I told you! It had nothing to do with her! It was just to get a few lousy dollars!

HUGO

Suddenly raises his head from his arms and, looking straight in front of him, pounds on the table frightenedly with his small fists.

Don't be a fool! Buy me a trink! But no more vine! It is not properly iced!

With guttural rage.

Gottamned stupid proletarian slaves! Buy me a trink or I vill have you shot!

He collapses into abject begging.

Please, for Gott's sake! I am not trunk enough! I cannot sleep! Life is a crazy monkey-face! Always there is blood beneath the villow trees! I hate it and I am afraid!

He hides his face on his arms, sobbing muffledly.

Please, I am crazy trunk! I say crazy things! For Gott's sake, do not listen to me!

But no one pays any attention to him. LARRY *stands shrunk back against*

the bar. ROCKY *is leaning over it. They stare at* HICKEY. PARRITT
stands looking pleadingly at LARRY.

HICKEY

Gazes with worried kindliness at HOPE.

You're beginning to worry me, Governor. Something's holding you
up somewhere. I don't see why— You've faced the truth about yourself. You've done what you had to do to kill your nagging pipe
dreams. Oh, I know it knocks you cold. But only for a minute. Then
you see it was the only possible way to peace. And you feel happy.
Like I did. That's what worries me about you, Governor. It's time
you began to feel happy—

CURTAIN

Act Four

Same as Act One—the back room with the curtain separating it from the section of the barroom with its single table at right of curtain, front. It is around half past one in the morning of the following day.

The tables in the back room have a new arrangement. The one at left, front, before the window to the yard, is in the same position. So is the one at the right, rear, of it in the second row. But this table now has only one chair. This chair is at right of it, facing directly front. The two tables on either side of the door at rear are unchanged. But the table which was at center, front, has been pushed toward right so that it and the table at right, rear, of it in the second row, and the last table at right in the front row, are now jammed so closely together that they form one group.

LARRY, HUGO and PARRITT are at the table at left, front. LARRY is at left of it, beside the window, facing front. HUGO sits at rear, facing front, his head on his arms in his habitual position, but he is not asleep. On HUGO's left is PARRITT, his chair facing left, front. At right of table, an empty chair, facing left. LARRY's chin is on his chest, his eyes fixed on the floor. He will not look at PARRITT, who keeps staring at him with a sneering, pleading challenge.

Two bottles of whiskey are on each table, whiskey and chaser glasses, a pitcher of water.

The one chair by the table at right, rear, of them is vacant.

At the first table at right of center, CORA sits at left, front, of it, facing front. Around the rear of this table are four empty chairs. Opposite

CORA, *in a sixth chair, is* CAPTAIN LEWIS, *also facing front. On his left,* MCGLOIN *is facing front in a chair before the middle table of his group. At right, rear, of him, also at this table,* GENERAL WETJOEN *sits facing front. In back of this table are three empty chairs.*

At right, rear, of WETJOEN, *but beside the last table of the group, sits* WILLIE. *On* WILLIE'S *left, at rear of table, is* HOPE. *On* HOPE'S *left, at right, rear, of table, is* MOSHER. *Finally, at right of table is* JIMMY TOMORROW. *All of the four sit facing front.*

There is an atmosphere of oppressive stagnation in the room, and a quality of insensibility about all the people in this group at right. They are like wax figures, set stiffly on their chairs, carrying out mechanically the motions of getting drunk but sunk in a numb stupor which is impervious to stimulation.

In the bar section, JOE *is sprawled in the chair at right of table, facing left. His head rolls forward in a sodden slumber.* ROCKY *is standing behind his chair, regarding him with dull hostility.* ROCKY'S *face is set in an expression of tired, callous toughness. He looks now like a minor Wop gangster.*

ROCKY
Shakes JOE *by the shoulder.*
Come on, yuh damned nigger! Beat it in de back room! It's after hours.
But JOE *remains inert.* ROCKY *gives up.*
Aw, to hell wid it. Let de dump get pinched. I'm through wid dis lousy job, anyway!
He hears someone at rear and calls.
Who's dat?
CHUCK *appears from rear. He has been drinking heavily, but there is no lift to his jag; his manner is grouchy and sullen. He has evidently been brawling. His knuckles are raw and there is a mouse under one eye. He has lost his straw hat, his tie is awry, and his blue suit is dirty.* ROCKY *eyes him indifferently.*

Been scrappin', huh? Started off on your periodical, ain't yuh?
For a second there is a gleam of satisfaction in his eyes.

CHUCK
Yeah, ain't yuh glad?
Truculently.
What's it to yuh?

ROCKY
Not a damn ting. But dis is someting to me. I'm out on my feet
holdin' down your job. Yuh said if I'd take your day, yuh'd relieve me
at six, and here it's half past one A.M. Well, yuh're takin' over now,
get me, no matter how plastered yuh are!

CHUCK
Plastered, hell! I wisht I was. I've lapped up a gallon, but it don't hit
me right. And to hell wid de job. I'm goin' to tell Harry I'm quittin'.

ROCKY
Yeah? Well, I'm quittin', too.

CHUCK
I've played sucker for dat crummy blonde long enough, lettin' her
kid me into woikin'. From now on I take it easy.

ROCKY
I'm glad yuh're gettin' some sense.

CHUCK
And I hope yuh're gettin' some. What a prize sap you been, tendin'
bar when yuh got two good hustlers in your stable!

ROCKY
Yea, but I ain't no sap now. I'll loin dem, when dey get back from
Coney.
Sneeringly.
Jees, dat Cora sure played you for a dope, feedin' yuh dat marriage-
on-de-farm hop!

CHUCK
Dully.

Yeah. Hickey got it right. A lousy pipe dream. It was her pulling sherry flips on me woke me up. All de way walkin' to de ferry, every ginmill we come to she'd drag me in to blow her. I got tinkin', Christ, what won't she want when she gets de ring on her finger and I'm hooked? So I tells her at de ferry, "Kiddo, yuh can go to Joisey, or to hell, but count me out."

ROCKY

She says it was her told you to go to hell, because yuh'd started hittin' de booze.

CHUCK

Ignoring this.

I got tinkin', too, Jees, won't I look sweet wid a wife dat if yuh put all de guys she's stayed wid side by side, dey'd reach to Chicago.

He sighs gloomily.

Dat kind of dame, yuh can't trust 'em. De minute your back is toined, dey're cheatin' wid de iceman or someone. Hickey done me a favor, makin' me wake up.

He pauses—then adds pathetically.

On'y it was fun, kinda, me and Cora kiddin' ourselves—

Suddenly his face hardens with hatred.

Where is dat son of a bitch, Hickey? I want one good sock at dat guy—just one!—and de next buttin' in he'll do will be in de morgue! I'll take a chance on goin' to de Chair—!

ROCKY

Starts—in a low warning voice.

Piano! Keep away from him, Chuck! He ain't here now, anyway. He went out to phone, he said. He wouldn't call from here. I got a hunch he's beat it. But if he does come back, yuh don't know him, if anyone asks yuh, get me?

As CHUCK *looks at him with dull surprise he lowers his voice to a whisper.*

De Chair, maybe dat's where he's goin'. I don't know nuttin', see, but it looks like he croaked his wife.

CHUCK

With a flash of interest.

Yuh mean she really was cheatin' on him? Den I don't blame de guy—

ROCKY

Who's blamin' him? When a dame asks for it— But I don't know nuttin' about it, see?

CHUCK

Is any of de gang wise?

ROCKY

Larry is. And de boss ought to be. I tried to wise de rest of dem up to stay clear of him, but dey're all so licked, I don't know if dey got it. *He pauses—vindictively.*
I don't give a damn what he done to his wife, but if he gets de Hot Seat I won't go into no mournin'!

CHUCK

Me, neider!

ROCKY

Not after his trowin' it in my face I'm a pimp. What if I am? Why de hell not? And what he's done to Harry. Jees, de poor old slob is so licked he can't even get drunk. And all de gang. Dey're all licked. I couldn't help feelin' sorry for de poor bums when dey showed up tonight, one by one, lookin' like pooches wid deir tails between deir legs, dat everyone'd been kickin' till dey was too punch-drunk to feel it no more. Jimmy Tomorrow was de last. Schwartz, de copper, brung him in. Seen him sittin' on de dock on West Street, lookin' at de water and cryin'! Schwartz thought he was drunk and I let him tink it. But he was cold sober. He was tryin' to jump in and didn't have de noive, I figgered it. Noive! Jees, dere ain't enough guts left in de whole gang to battle a mosquito!

CHUCK

Aw, to hell wid 'em! Who cares? Gimme a drink.
ROCKY *pushes the bottle toward him apathetically.*
I see you been hittin' de redeye, too.

ROCKY

Yeah. But it don't do no good. I can't get drunk right.

CHUCK *drinks.* JOE *mumbles in his sleep.* CHUCK *regards him resentfully.*

Dis doity dinge was able to get his snootful and pass out. Jees, even Hickey can't faze a nigger! Yuh'd tink he was fazed if yuh'd seen him come in. Stinko, and he pulled a gat and said he'd plug Hickey for insultin' him. Den he dropped it and begun to cry and said he wasn't a gamblin' man or a tough guy no more; he was yellow. He'd borrowed de gat to stick up someone, and den didn't have de guts. He got drunk panhandlin' drinks in nigger joints, I s'pose. I guess dey felt sorry for him.

CHUCK

He ain't got no business in de bar after hours. Why don't yuh chuck him out?

ROCKY

Apathetically.

Aw, to hell wid it. Who cares?

CHUCK

Lapsing into the same mood.

Yeah. I don't.

JOE

Suddenly lunges to his feet dazedly—mumbles in humbled apology.

Scuse me, White Boys. Scuse me for livin'. I don't want to be where I's not wanted.

He makes his way swayingly to the opening in the curtain at rear and tacks down to the middle table of the three at right, front. He feels his way around it to the table at its left and gets to the chair in back of CAPTAIN LEWIS.

CHUCK

Gets up—in a callous, brutal tone.

My pig's in de back room, ain't she? I wanna collect de dough I wouldn't take dis mornin', like a sucker, before she blows it.

He goes rear.

ROCKY

Getting up.

I'm comin', too. I'm trough woikin'. I ain't no lousy bartender.

CHUCK *comes through the curtain and looks for* CORA *as* JOE *flops down in the chair in back of* CAPTAIN LEWIS.

JOE

Taps LEWIS *on the shoulder—servilely apologetic.*

If you objects to my sittin' here, Captain, just tell me and I pulls my freight.

LEWIS

No apology required, old chap. Anybody could tell you I should feel honored a bloody Kaffir would lower himself to sit beside me.

JOE *stares at him with sodden perplexity—then closes his eyes.* CHUCK *comes forward to take the chair behind* CORA's, *as* ROCKY *enters the back room and starts over toward* LARRY's *table.*

CHUCK

His voice hard.

I'm waitin', Baby. Dig!

CORA

With apathetic obedience.

Sure. I been expectin' yuh. I got it all ready. Here.

She passes a small roll of bills she has in her hand over her shoulder, without looking at him. He takes it, glances at it suspiciously, then shoves it in his pocket without a word of acknowledgment. CORA *speaks with a tired wonder at herself rather than resentment toward him.*

Jees, imagine me kiddin' myself I wanted to marry a drunken pimp.

CHUCK

Dat's nuttin', Baby. Imagine de sap I'da been, when I can get your dough just as easy widout it!

ROCKY

Takes the chair on PARRITT's *left, facing* LARRY—*dully.*

Hello, Old Cemetery.

LARRY *doesn't seem to hear. To* PARRITT.

Hello, Tightwad. You still around?

PARRITT

Keeps his eyes on LARRY—*in a jeeringly challenging tone.*

Ask Larry! He knows I'm here, all right, although he's pretending not to! He'd like to forget I'm alive! He's trying to kid himself with that grandstand philosopher stuff! But he knows he can't get away with it now! He kept himself locked in his room until a while ago, alone with a bottle of booze, but he couldn't make it work! He couldn't even get drunk! He had to come out! There must have been something there he was even more scared to face than he is Hickey and me! I guess he got looking at the fire escape and thinking how handy it was, if he was really sick of life and only had the nerve to die!

He pauses sneeringly. LARRY'S *face has tautened, but he pretends he doesn't hear.* ROCKY *pays no attention. His head has sunk forward, and he stares at the table top, sunk in the same stupor as the other occupants of the room.* PARRITT *goes on, his tone becoming more insistent.*

He's been thinking of me, too, Rocky. Trying to figure a way to get out of helping me! He doesn't want to be bothered understanding. But he does understand all right! He used to love her, too. So he thinks I ought to take a hop off the fire escape!

He pauses. LARRY'S *hands on the table have clinched into fists, as his nails dig into his palms, but he remains silent.* PARRITT *breaks and starts pleading.*

For God's sake, Larry, can't you say something? Hickey's got me all balled up. Thinking of what he must have done has got me so I don't know any more what I did or why. I can't go on like this! I've got to know what I ought to do—

LARRY

In a stifled tone.

God damn you! Are you trying to make me your executioner?

PARRITT

Starts frightenedly.

Execution? then you do think—?

LARRY

I don't think anything!

185

PARRITT

With forced jeering.

I suppose you think I ought to die because I sold out a lot of loud-mouthed fakers, who were cheating suckers with a phony pipe dream, and put them where they ought to be, in jail?

He forces a laugh.

Don't make me laugh! I ought to get a medal! What a damned old sap you are! You must still believe in the Movement!

He nudges ROCKY *with his elbow.*

Hickey's right about him, isn't he, Rocky? An old no-good drunken tramp, as dumb as he is, ought to take a hop off the fire escape!

ROCKY

Dully.

Sure. Why don't he? Or you? Or me? What de hell's de difference? Who cares?

There is a faint stir from all the crowd, as if this sentiment struck a responsive chord in their numbed minds. They mumble almost in chorus as one voice, like sleepers talking out of a dully irritating dream, "The hell with it!" "Who cares?" Then the sodden silence descends again on the room. ROCKY *looks from* PARRITT *to* LARRY *puzzledly. He mutters.*

What am I doin' here wid youse two? I remember I had someting on my mind to tell yuh. What—? Oh, I got it now.

He looks from one to the other of their oblivious faces with a strange, sly, calculating look—ingratiatingly.

I was tinking how you was bot' reg'lar guys. I tinks, ain't two guys like dem saps to be hangin' round like a coupla stew bums and wastin' demselves. Not dat I blame yuh for not woikin'. On'y suckers woik. But dere's no percentage in bein' broke when yuh can grab good jack for yourself and make someone else woik for yuh, is dere? I mean, like I do. So I tinks, Dey're my pals and I ought to wise up two good guys like dem to play my system, and not be lousy barflies, no good to demselves or nobody else.

He addresses PARRITT *now—persuasively.*

What yuh tink, Parritt? Ain't I right? Sure, I am. So don't be a sucker, see? Yuh ain't a bad-lookin' guy. Yuh could easy make some gal who's a good hustler, an' start a stable. I'd help yuh and wise yuh up to de inside dope on de game.

He pauses inquiringly. PARRITT *gives no sign of having heard him.* ROCKY *asks impatiently.*

Well, what about it? What if dey do call yuh a pimp? What de hell do you care—any more'n I do.

PARRITT

Without looking at him—vindictively.

I'm through with whores. I wish they were all in jail—or dead!

ROCKY

Ignores this—disappointedly.

So yuh won't touch it, huh? Aw right, stay a bum!

He turns to LARRY.

Jees, Larry, he's sure one dumb boob, ain't he? Dead from de neck up! He don't know a good ting when he sees it.

Oily, even persuasive again.

But how about you, Larry? You ain't dumb. So why not, huh? Sure, yuh're old, but dat don't matter. All de hustlers tink yuh're aces. Dey fall for yuh like yuh was deir uncle or old man or someting. Dey'd like takin' care of yuh. And de cops 'round here, dey like yuh, too. It'd be a pipe for yuh, 'specially wid me to help yuh and wise yuh up. Yuh wouldn't have to worry where de next drink's comin' from, or wear doity clothes.

Hopefully.

Well, don't it look good to yuh?

LARRY

Glances at him—for a moment he is stirred to sardonic pity.

No, it doesn't look good, Rocky. I mean, the peace Hickey's brought you. It isn't contented enough, if you have to make everyone else a pimp, too.

ROCKY

Stares at him stupidly—then pushes his chair back and gets up, grumbling.

I'm a sap to waste time on yuh. A stew bum is a stew bum and yuh can't change him.

He turns away—then turns back for an afterthought.

Like I was sayin' to Chuck, yuh better keep away from Hickey. If anyone asks yuh, yuh don't know nuttin', get me? Yuh never even hoid he had a wife.

His face hardens.

Jees, we all ought to git drunk and stage a celebration when dat bastard goes to de Chair.

LARRY

Vindictively.

Be God, I'll celebrate with you and drink long life to him in hell!

Then guiltily and pityingly.

No! The poor mad devil—

Then with angry self-contempt.

Ah, pity again! The wrong kind! He'll welcome the Chair!

PARRITT

Contemptuously.

Yes, what are you so damned scared of death for? I don't want your lousy pity.

ROCKY

Christ, I hope he don't come back, Larry. We don't know nuttin' now. We're on'y guessin', see? But if de bastard keeps on talkin'—

LARRY

Grimly.

He'll come back. He'll keep on talking. He's got to. He's lost his confidence that the peace he's sold us is the real McCoy, and it's made him uneasy about his own. He'll have to prove to us—

As he is speaking HICKEY *appears silently in the doorway at rear. He has lost his beaming salesman's grin. His manner is no longer self-assured. His expression is uneasy, baffled and resentful. It has the stubborn set of an obsessed determination. His eyes are on* LARRY *as he comes in. As he speaks, there is a start from all the crowd, a shrinking away from him.*

HICKEY

Angrily.

That's a damned lie, Larry! I haven't lost confidence a damned bit!
Why should I?
Boastfully.
By God, whenever I made up my mind to sell someone something
I knew they ought to want, I've sold 'em!
He suddenly looks confused—haltingly.
I mean— It isn't kind of you, Larry, to make that kind of crack when
I've been doing my best to help—

ROCKY

Moving away from him toward right—sharply.
Keep away from me! I don't know nuttin' about yuh, see?
*His tone is threatening but his manner as he turns his back and ducks
quickly across to the bar entrance is that of one in flight. In the bar he
comes forward and slumps in a chair at the table, facing front.*

HICKEY

Comes to the table at right, rear, of LARRY's *table and sits in the one
chair there, facing front. He looks over the crowd at right, hopefully and
then disappointedly. He speaks with a strained attempt at his old affectionate jollying manner.*
Well, well! How are you coming along, everybody? Sorry I had to
leave you for a while, but there was something I had to get finally
settled. It's all fixed now.

HOPE

In the voice of one reiterating mechanically a hopeless complaint.
When are you going to do something about this booze, Hickey?
Bejees, we all know you did something to take the life out of it. It's
like drinking dishwater! We can't pass out! And you promised us
peace.
*His group all join in in a dull, complaining chorus, "We can't pass out!
You promised us peace!"*

HICKEY

Bursts into resentful exasperation.
For God's sake, Harry, are you still harping on that damned nonsense! You've kept it up all afternoon and night! And you've got

everybody else singing the same crazy tune! I've had about all I can stand— That's why I phoned—

He controls himself.

Excuse me, boys and girls. I don't mean that. I'm just worried about you, when you play dead on me like this. I was hoping by the time I got back you'd be like you ought to be! I thought you were deliberately holding back, while I was around, because you didn't want to give me the satisfaction of showing me I'd had the right dope. And I did have! I know from my own experience.

Exasperatedly.

But I've explained that a million times! And you've all done what you needed to do! By rights you should be contented now, without a single damned hope or lying dream left to torment you! But here you are, acting like a lot of stiffs cheating the undertaker!

He looks around accusingly.

I can't figure it—unless it's just your damned pigheaded stubbornness!

He breaks— miserably.

Hell, you oughtn't to act this way with me! You're my old pals, the only friends I've got. You know the one thing I want is to see you all happy before I go—

Rousing himself to his old brisk, master-of-ceremonies manner.

And there's damned little time left now. I've made a date for two o'clock. We've got to get busy right away and find out what's wrong.

There is a sodden silence. He goes on exasperatedly.

Can't you appreciate what you've got, for God's sake? Don't you know you're free now to be yourselves, without having to feel remorse or guilt, or lie to yourselves about reforming tomorrow? Can't you see there is no tomorrow now? You're rid of it forever! You've killed it! You don't have to care a damn about anything any more! You've finally got the game of life licked, don't you see that?

Angrily exhorting.

Then why the hell don't you get pie-eyed and celebrate? Why don't you laugh and sing "Sweet Adeline"?

With bitterly hurt accusation.

The only reason I can think of is, you're putting on this rotten half-dead act just to get back at me! Because you hate my guts!

He breaks again.

God, don't do that, gang! It makes me feel like hell to think you hate me. It makes me feel you suspect I must have hated you. But that's a lie! Oh, I know I used to hate everyone in the world who wasn't as rotten a bastard as I was! But that was when I was still living in hell—before I faced the truth and saw the one possible way to free poor Evelyn and give her the peace she'd always dreamed about.

He pauses. Everyone in the group stirs with awakening dread and they all begin to grow tense on their chairs.

CHUCK

Without looking at HICKEY—*with dull, resentful viciousness.*

Aw, put a bag over it! To hell wid Evelyn! What if she was cheatin'? And who cares what yuh did to her? Dat's your funeral. We don't give a damn, see?

There is a dull, resentful chorus of assent, "We don't give a damn." CHUCK *adds dully.*

All we want outa you is keep de hell away from us and give us a rest.

A muttered chorus of assent.

HICKEY

As if he hadn't heard this—an obsessed look on his face.

The one possible way to make up to her for all I'd made her go through, and get her rid of me so I couldn't make her suffer any more, and she wouldn't have to forgive me again! I saw I couldn't do it by killing myself, like I wanted to for a long time. That would have been the last straw for her. She'd have died of a broken heart to think I could do that to her. She'd have blamed herself for it, too. Or I couldn't just run away from her. She'd have died of grief and humiliation if I'd done that to her. She'd have thought I'd stopped loving her.

He adds with a strange impressive simplicity.

You see, Evelyn loved me. And I loved her. That was the trouble. It would have been easy to find a way out if she hadn't loved me so much. Or if I hadn't loved her. But as it was, there was only one possible way.

He pauses—then adds simply.

I had to kill her.

There is a second's dead silence as he finishes—then a tense indrawn breath like a gasp from the crowd, and a general shrinking movement.

LARRY
Bursts out.
You mad fool, can't you keep your mouth shut! We may hate you for what you've done here this time, but we remember the old times, too, when you brought kindness and laughter with you instead of death! We don't want to know things that will make us help send you to the Chair!

PARRITT
With angry scorn.
Ah, shut up, you yellow faker! Can't you face anything? Wouldn't I deserve the Chair, too, if I'd— It's worse if you kill someone and they have to go on living. I'd be glad of the Chair! It'd wipe it out! It'd square me with myself!

HICKEY
Disturbed—with a movement of repulsion.
I wish you'd get rid of that bastard, Larry. I can't have him pretending there's something in common between him and me. It's what's in your heart that counts. There was love in my heart, not hate.

PARRITT
Glares at him in angry terror.
You're a liar! I don't hate her! I couldn't! And it had nothing to do with her, anyway! You ask Larry!

LARRY
Grabs his shoulder and shakes him furiously.
God damn you, stop shoving your rotten soul in my lap!
PARRITT *subsides, hiding his face in his hands and shuddering.*

HICKEY
Goes on quietly now.
Don't worry about the Chair, Larry. I know it's still hard for you not to be terrified by death, but when you've made peace with yourself, like I have, you won't give a damn.

He addresses the group at right again—earnestly.

Listen, everybody. I've made up my mind the only way I can clear things up for you, so you'll realize how contented and carefree you ought to feel, now I've made you get rid of your pipe dreams, is to show you what a pipe dream did to me and Evelyn. I'm certain if I tell you about it from the beginning, you'll appreciate what I've done for you and why I did it, and how damned grateful you ought to be—instead of hating me.

He begins eagerly in a strange running narrative manner.

You see, even when we were kids, Evelyn and me—

HOPE

Bursts out, pounding with his glass on the table.

No! Who the hell cares? We don't want to hear it. All we want is to pass out and get drunk and a little peace!

They are all, except LARRY and PARRITT, seized by the same fit and pound with their glasses, even HUGO, and ROCKY in the bar, and shout in chorus, "Who the hell cares? We want to pass out!"

HICKEY

With an expression of wounded hurt.

All right, if that's the way you feel. I don't want to cram it down your throats. I don't need to tell anyone. I don't feel guilty. I'm only worried about you.

HOPE

What did you do to this booze? That's what we'd like to hear. Bejees, you done something. There's no life or kick in it now.

He appeals mechanically to JIMMY TOMORROW.

Ain't that right, Jimmy?

JIMMY

More than any of them, his face has a wax-figure blankness that makes it look embalmed. He answers in a precise, completely lifeless voice, but his reply is not to HARRY's question, and he does not look at him or anyone else.

Yes. Quite right. It was all a stupid lie—my nonsense about tomorrow. Naturally, they would never give me my position back. I would never dream of asking them. It would be hopeless. I didn't resign. I was fired for drunkenness. And that was years ago. I'm much worse now. And it was absurd of me to excuse my drunkenness by pretending it was my wife's adultery that ruined my life. As Hickey guessed, I was a drunkard before that. Long before. I discovered early in life that living frightened me when I was sober. I have forgotten why I married Marjorie. I can't even remember now if she was pretty. She was a blonde, I think, but I couldn't swear to it. I had some idea of wanting a home, perhaps. But, of course, I much preferred the nearest pub. Why Marjorie married me, God knows. It's impossible to believe she loved me. She soon found I much preferred drinking all night with my pals to being in bed with her. So, naturally, she was unfaithful. I didn't blame her. I really didn't care. I was glad to be free—even grateful to her, I think, for giving me such a good tragic excuse to drink as much as I damned well pleased.

He stops like a mechanical doll that has run down. No one gives any sign of having heard him. There is a heavy silence. Then ROCKY, *at the table in the bar, turns grouchily as he hears a noise behind him. Two men come quietly forward. One,* MORAN, *is middle-aged. The other,* LIEB, *is in his twenties. They look ordinary in every way, without anything distinctive to indicate what they do for a living.*

ROCKY
Grumpily.
In de back room if yuh wanta drink.

MORAN *makes a peremptory sign to be quiet. All of a sudden* ROCKY *senses they are detectives and springs up to face them, his expression freezing into a wary blankness.* MORAN *pulls back his coat to show his badge.*

MORAN
In a low voice.
Guy named Hickman in the back room?

ROCKY
Tink I know de names of all de guys—?

MORAN
Listen, you! This is murder. And don't be a sap. It was Hickman himself phoned in and said we'd find him here around two.

ROCKY

Dully.

So dat's who he phoned to.

He shrugs his shoulders.

Aw right, if he asked for it. He's de fat guy sittin' alone.

He slumps down in his chair again.

And if yuh want a confession all yuh got to do is listen. He'll be tellin' all about it soon. Yuh can't stop de bastard talkin'.

MORAN *gives him a curious look, then whispers to* LIEB, *who disappears rear and a moment later appears in the hall doorway of the back room. He spots* HICKEY *and slides into a chair at the left of the doorway, cutting off escape by the hall.* MORAN *goes back and stands in the opening in the curtain leading to the back room. He sees* HICKEY *and stands watching him and listening.*

HICKEY

Suddenly bursts out.

I've got to tell you! Your being the way you are now gets my goat! It's all wrong! It puts things in my mind—about myself. It makes me think, if I got balled up about you, how do I know I wasn't balled up about myself? And that's plain damned foolishness. When you know the story of me and Evelyn, you'll see there wasn't any other possible way out of it, for her sake. Only I've got to start way back at the beginning or you won't understand.

He starts his story, his tone again becoming musingly reminiscent.

You see, even as a kid I was always restless. I had to keep on the go. You've heard the old saying, "Ministers' sons are sons of guns." Well, that was me, and then some. Home was like a jail. I didn't fall for the religious bunk. Listening to my old man whooping up hell fire and scaring those Hoosier suckers into shelling out their dough only handed me a laugh, although I had to hand it to him, the way he sold them nothing for something. I guess I take after him, and that's what made me a good salesman. Well, anyway, as I said, home was like jail, and so was school, and so was that damned hick town. The only place I liked was the pool rooms, where I could smoke Sweet Caporals, and mop up a couple of beers, thinking I was a hell-on-wheels sport. We had one hooker shop in town, and, of course, I liked that, too. Not that I hardly ever had entrance money. My old man was a tight old bastard. But I liked to sit around in the parlor and joke with the girls, and they liked me because I could kid 'em along and make 'em laugh. Well, you know what a small town is. Everyone got wise to me. They all said I was a no-good tramp. I didn't give a damn what they said. I hated everybody in the place. That is, except Evelyn. I loved Evelyn. Even as a kid. And Evelyn loved me.

He pauses. No one moves or gives any sign except by the dread in their eyes that they have heard him. Except PARRITT, *who takes his hands from his face to look at* LARRY *pleadingly.*

PARRITT

I loved Mother, Larry! No matter what she did! I still do! Even though I know she wishes now I was dead! You believe that, don't you? Christ, why can't you say something?

HICKEY

Too absorbed in his story now to notice this—goes on in a tone of fond, sentimental reminiscence.

Yes, sir, as far back as I can remember, Evelyn and I loved each other. She always stuck up for me. She wouldn't believe the gossip—or she'd pretend she didn't. No one could convince her I was no good. Evelyn was stubborn as all hell once she'd made up her mind. Even when I'd admit things and ask her forgiveness, she'd make excuses for me and defend me against myself. She'd kiss me and say she knew I didn't mean it and I wouldn't do it again. So I'd promise I wouldn't. I'd have to promise, she was so sweet and good, though I knew darned well—

A touch of strange bitterness comes into his voice for a moment.

No, sir, you couldn't stop Evelyn. Nothing on earth could shake her faith in me. Even I couldn't. She was a sucker for a pipe dream.

Then quickly.

Well, naturally, her family forbid her seeing me. They were one of the town's best, rich for that hick burg, owned the trolley line and lumber company. Strict Methodists, too. They hated my guts. But they couldn't stop Evelyn. She'd sneak notes to me and meet me on the sly. I was getting more restless. The town was getting more like a jail. I made up my mind to beat it. I knew exactly what I wanted to be by that time. I'd met a lot of drummers around the hotel and liked 'em. They were always telling jokes. They were sports. They kept moving. I liked their life. And I knew I could kid people and sell things. The hitch was how to get the railroad fare to the Big Town. I told Mollie Arlington my trouble. She was the madame of the cathouse. She liked me. She laughed and said, "Hell, I'll stake you, Kid! I'll bet on you. With that grin of yours and that line of bull, you ought to be able to sell skunks for good ratters!"

He chuckles.

Mollie was all right. She gave me confidence in myself. I paid her back, the first money I earned. Wrote her a kidding letter, I remember, saying I was peddling baby carriages and she and the girls had better take advantage of our bargain offer.

He chuckles.

But that's ahead of my story. The night before I left town, I had a date with Evelyn. I got all worked up, she was so pretty and sweet and good. I told her straight, "You better forget me, Evelyn, for your own sake. I'm no good and never will be. I'm not worthy to wipe your shoes." I broke down and cried. She just said, looking white and scared, "Why, Teddy? Don't you still love me?" I said, "Love you? God, Evelyn, I love you more than anything in the world. And I always will!" She said, "Then nothing else matters, Teddy, because nothing but death could stop my loving you. So I'll wait, and when you're ready you send for me and we'll be married. I know I can make you happy, Teddy, and once you're happy you won't want to do any of the bad things you've done any more." And I said, "Of course, I won't, Evelyn!" I meant it, too. I believed it. I loved her so much she could make me believe anything.

He sighs. There is a suspended, waiting silence. Even the two detectives are drawn into it. Then HOPE *breaks into dully exasperated, brutally callous protest.*

HOPE

Get it over, you long-winded bastard! You married her, and you caught her cheating with the iceman, and you croaked her, and who the hell cares? What's she to us? All we want is to pass out in peace, bejees!

A chorus of dull, resentful protest from all the group. They mumble, like sleepers who curse a person who keeps awakening them, "What's it to us? We want to pass out in peace!" HOPE *drinks and they mechanically follow his example. He pours another and they do the same. He complains with a stupid, nagging insistence.*

No life in the booze! No kick! Dishwater. Bejees, I'll never pass out!

HICKEY

Goes on as if there had been no interruption.

So I beat it to the Big Town. I got a job easy, and it was a cinch for me to make good. I had the knack. It was like a game, sizing people up quick, spotting what their pet pipe dreams were, and then kidding 'em along that line, pretending you believed what they wanted to believe about themselves. Then they liked you, they trusted you, they wanted to buy something to show their gratitude. It was fun. But still, all the while I felt guilty, as if I had no right to be having such a good time away from Evelyn. In each letter I'd tell her how I missed her, but I'd keep warning her, too. I'd tell her all my faults, how I liked my booze every once in a while, and so on. But there was no shaking Evelyn's belief in me, or her dreams about the future. After each letter of hers, I'd be as full of faith as she was. So as soon as I got enough saved to start us off, I sent for her and we got married. Christ, wasn't I happy for a while! And wasn't she happy! I don't care what anyone says, I'll bet there never was two people who loved each other more than me and Evelyn. Not only then but always after, in spite of everything I did—

He pauses—then sadly.

Well, it's all there, at the start, everything that happened afterwards. I never could learn to handle temptation. I'd want to reform and mean it. I'd promise Evelyn, and I'd promise myself, and I'd believe it. I'd tell her, it's the last time. And she'd say, "I know it's the last time, Teddy. You'll never do it again." That's what made it so hard. That's what made me feel such a rotten skunk—her always forgiving me. My playing around with women, for instance. It was only a harmless good time to me. Didn't mean anything. But I'd know what it meant to Evelyn. So I'd say to myself, never again. But you know how it is, traveling around. The damned hotel rooms. I'd get seeing things in the wall paper. I'd get bored as hell. Lonely and homesick. But at the same time sick of home. I'd feel free and I'd want to celebrate a little. I never drank on the job, so it had to be dames. Any tart. What I'd want was some tramp I could be myself with without being ashamed—someone I could tell a dirty joke to and she'd laugh.

CORA

With a dull, weary bitterness.

Jees, all de lousy jokes I've had to listen to and pretend was funny!

HICKEY

Goes on obliviously.

Sometimes I'd try some joke I thought was a corker on Evelyn. She'd always make herself laugh. But I could tell she though it was dirty, not funny. And Evelyn always knew about the tarts I'd been with when I came home from a trip. She'd kiss me and look in my eyes, and she'd know. I'd see in her eyes how she was trying not to know, and then telling herself even if it was true, he couldn't help it, they tempt him, and he's lonely, he hasn't got me, it's only his body, anyway, he doesn't love them, I'm the only one he loves. She was right, too. I never loved anyone else. Couldn't if I wanted to.

He pauses.

She forgave me even when it all had to come out in the open. You know how it is when you keep taking chances. You may be lucky for a long time, but you get nicked in the end. I picked up a nail from some tart in Altoona.

CORA

Dully, without resentment.

Yeah. And she picked it up from some guy. It's all in de game. What de hell of it?

HICKEY

I had to do a lot of lying and stalling when I got home. It didn't do any good. The quack I went to got all my dough and then told me I was cured and I took his word. But I wasn't, and poor Evelyn—

But she did her best to make me believe she fell for my lie about how traveling men get things from drinking cups on trains. Anyway, she forgave me. The same way she forgave me every time I'd turn up after a periodical drunk. You all know what I'd be like at the end of one. You've seen me. Like something lying in the gutter that no alley cat would lower itself to drag in—something they threw out of the D.T. ward in Bellevue along with the garbage, something that ought to be dead and isn't!

His face is convulsed with self-loathing.

Evelyn wouldn't have heard from me in a month or more. She'd have been waiting there alone, with the neighbors shaking their heads and feeling sorry for her out loud. That was before she got me to move to the outskirts, where there weren't any next-door neighbors. And then the door would open and in I'd stumble—looking like what I've said—into her home, where she kept everything so spotless and clean. And I'd sworn it would never happen again, and now I'd have to start swearing again this was the last time. I could see disgust having a battle in her eyes with love. Love always won. She'd make herself kiss me, as if nothing had happened, as if I'd just come home from a business trip. She'd never complain or bawl me out.

He bursts out in a tone of anguish that has anger and hatred beneath it.

Christ, can you imagine what a guilty skunk she made me feel! If she'd only admitted once she didn't believe any more in her pipe dream that some day I'd behave! But she never would. Evelyn was stubborn as hell. Once she'd set her heart on anything, you couldn't shake her faith that it had to come true—tomorrow! It was the same old story, over and over, for years and years. It kept piling up, inside her and inside me. God, can you picture all I made her suffer, and all the guilt she made me feel, and how I hated myself! If she only hadn't been so damned good—if she'd been the same kind of wife I was a husband. God, I used to pray sometimes she'd—I'd even say to her, "Go on, why don't you, Evelyn? It'd serve me right. I wouldn't mind. I'd forgive you." Of course, I'd pretend I was kidding—the same way I used to joke here about her being in the hay with the iceman. She'd have been so hurt if I'd said it seriously. She'd have thought I'd stopped loving her.

He pauses—then looking around at them.

I suppose you think I'm a liar, that no woman could have stood all she stood and still loved me so much—that it isn't human for any woman to be so pitying and forgiving. Well, I'm not lying, and if you'd ever seen her, you'd realize I wasn't. It was written all over her face, sweetness and love and pity and forgiveness.

He reaches mechanically for the inside pocket of his coat.

Wait! I'll show you. I always carry her picture.

Suddenly he looks startled. He stares before him, his hand falling back—quietly.

No, I'm forgetting I tore it up—afterwards. I didn't need it any more.

He pauses. The silence is like that in the room of a dying man where people hold their breath, waiting for him to die.

CORA

With a muffled sob.

Jees, Hickey! Jees!

She shivers and puts her hands over her face.

PARRITT

To LARRY *in a low insistent tone.*

I burnt up Mother's picture, Larry. Her eyes followed me all the time. They seemed to be wishing I was dead!

HICKEY

It kept piling up, like I've said. I got so I thought of it all the time. I hated myself more and more, thinking of all the wrong I'd done to the sweetest woman in the world who loved me so much. I got so I'd curse myself for a lousy bastard every time I saw myself in the mirror. I felt such pity for her it drove me crazy. You wouldn't believe a guy like me, that's knocked around so much, could feel such pity. It got so every night I'd wind up hiding my face in her lap, bawling and begging her forgiveness. And, of course, she'd always comfort me and say, "Never mind, Teddy, I know you won't ever again." Christ, I loved her so, but I began to hate that pipe dream! I began to be afraid I was going bughouse, because sometimes I couldn't forgive her for forgiving me. I even caught myself hating her for making me hate myself so much. There's a limit to the guilt you can feel and the forgiveness and the pity you can take! You have to begin blaming someone else, too. I got so sometimes when she'd kiss me it was like she did it on purpose to humiliate me, as if she'd spit in my face! But all the time I saw how crazy and rotten of me that was, and it made me hate myself all the more. You'd never believe I could hate so much, a good-natured, happy-go-lucky slob like me. And as the time got nearer to when I was due to come here for my drunk around Harry's birthday, I got nearly crazy. I kept swearing to her every night that this time I really wouldn't, until I'd made it a real final test to myself—and to her. And she kept encouraging me and saying, "I can see you really mean it now, Teddy. I know you'll conquer it this time, and we'll be so happy, dear." When she'd say that and kiss me, I'd believe it, too. Then she'd go to bed, and I'd stay up alone because I couldn't sleep and I didn't want to disturb her, tossing and rolling around. I'd get so damned lonely. I'd get thinking how peaceful it was here, sitting around with the old gang, getting drunk and forgetting love, joking and laughing and singing and swapping lies. And finally I knew I'd have to come. And I knew if I came this time, it was the finish. I'd never have the guts to go back and be forgiven again, and that would break Evelyn's heart because to her it would mean I didn't love her any more.

He pauses.

That last night I'd driven myself crazy trying to figure some way out for her. I went in the bedroom. I was going to tell her it was the end. But I couldn't do that to her. She was sound asleep. I thought, God, if she'd only never wake up, she'd never know! And then it came to me—the only possible way out, for her sake. I remembered I'd given her a gun for protection while I was away and it was in the bureau drawer. She'd never feel any pain, never wake up from her dream. So I—

HOPE

Tries to ward this off by pounding with his glass on the table—with brutal, callous exasperation.

Give us a rest, for the love of Christ! Who the hell cares? We want to pass out in peace!

They all, except PARRITT *and* LARRY, *pound with their glasses and grumble in chorus: "Who the hell cares? We want to pass out in peace!"* MORAN, *the detective, moves quietly from the entrance in the curtain across the back of the room to the table where his companion,* LIEB, *is sitting.* ROCKY *notices his leaving and gets up from the table in the rear and goes back to stand and watch in the entrance.* MORAN *exchanges a glance with* LIEB, *motioning him to get up. The latter does so. No one notices them. The clamor of banging glasses dies out as abruptly as it started.* HICKEY *hasn't appeared to hear it.*

HICKEY
Simply.
So I killed her.
There is a moment of dead silence. Even the detectives are caught in it and stand motionless.

PARRITT
Suddenly gives up and relaxes limply in his chair—in a low voice in which there is a strange exhausted relief.
I may as well confess, Larry. There's no use lying any more. You know, anyway. I didn't give a damn about the money. It was because I hated her.

HICKEY
Obliviously.
And then I saw I'd always known that was the only possible way to give her peace and free her from the misery of loving me. I saw it meant peace for me, too, knowing she was at peace. I felt as though a ton of guilt was lifted off my mind. I remember I stood by the bed and suddenly I had to laugh. I couldn't help it, and I knew Evelyn would forgive me. I remember I heard myself speaking to her, as if it was something I'd always wanted to say: "Well, you know what you can do with your pipe dream now, you damned bitch!"
He stops with a horrified start, as if shocked out of a nightmare, as if he couldn't believe he heard what he had just said. He stammers.
No! I never—!

PARRITT

To LARRY—*sneeringly.*

Yes, that's it! Her and the damned old Movement pipe dream! Eh, Larry?

HICKEY

Bursts into frantic denial.

No! That's a lie! I never said—! Good God, I couldn't have said that! If I did, I'd gone insane! Why, I loved Evelyn better than anything in life!

He appeals brokenly to the crowd.

Boys, you're all my old pals! You've known old Hickey for years! You know I'd never—

His eyes fix on HOPE.

You've known me longer than anyone, Harry. You know I must have been insane, don't you, Governor?

HOPE

At first with the same defensive callousness—without looking at him.

Who the hell cares?

Then suddenly he looks at HICKEY *and there is an extraordinary change in his expression. His face lights up, as if he were grasping at some dawning hope in his mind. He speaks with a groping eagerness.*

Insane? You mean—you went really insane?

At the tone of his voice, all the group at the tables by him start and stare at him as if they caught his thought. Then they all look at HICKEY *eagerly, too.*

HICKEY

Yes! Or I couldn't have laughed! I couldn't have said that to her!

MORAN *walks up behind him on one side, while the second detective,* LIEB, *closes in on him from the other.*

MORAN

Taps HICKEY *on the shoulder.*

That's enough, Hickman. You know who we are. You're under arrest.

He nods to LIEB, *who slips a pair of handcuffs on* HICKEY's *wrists.* HICKEY *stares at them with stupid incomprehension.* MORAN *takes his arm.*

Come along and spill your guts where we can get it on paper.

HICKEY

No, wait, Officer! You owe me a break! I phoned and made it easy
for you, didn't I? Just a few minutes!
To HOPE—*pleadingly.*
You know I couldn't say that to Evelyn, don't you, Harry—unless—

HOPE

Eagerly.
And you've been crazy ever since? Everything you've said and done
here—

HICKEY

*For a moment forgets his own obsession and his face takes on its familiar
expression of affectionate amusement and he chuckles.*
Now, Governor! Up to your old tricks, eh? I see what you're driving
at, but I can't let you get away with—
Then, as HOPE'S *expression turns to resentful callousness again and he
looks away, he adds hastily with pleading desperation.*
Yes, Harry, of course, I've been out of my mind ever since! All the
time I've been here! You saw I was insane, didn't you?

MORAN

With cynical disgust.
Can it! I've had enough of your act. Save it for the jury.
Addressing the crowd, sharply.
Listen, you guys. Don't fall for his lies. He's starting to get foxy now
and thinks he'll plead insanity. But he can't get away with it.
*The crowd at the grouped tables are grasping at hope now. They glare at
him resentfully.*

HOPE

Begins to bristle in his old-time manner.
Bejees, you dumb dick, you've got a crust trying to tell us about
Hickey! We've known him for years, and every one of us noticed
he was nutty the minute he showed up here! Bejees, if you'd heard
all the crazy bull he was pulling about bringing us peace—like a
bughouse preacher escaped from an asylum! If you'd seen all the
damned-fool things he made us do! We only did them because—

He hesitates—then defiantly.

Because we hoped he'd come out of it if we kidded him along and humored him.

He looks around at the others.

Ain't that right, fellers?

They burst into a chorus of eager assent: "Yes, Harry!" "That's it, Harry!" "That's why!" "We knew he was crazy!" "Just to humor him!"

MORAN

A fine bunch of rats! Covering up for a dirty, cold-blooded murderer.

HOPE

Stung into recovering all his old fuming truculence.

Is that so? Bejees, you know the old story, when Saint Patrick drove the snakes out of Ireland they swam to New York and joined the police force! Ha!

He cackles insultingly.

Bejees, we can believe it now when we look at you, can't we, fellers?

They all growl assent, glowering defiantly at MORAN. MORAN *glares at them, looking as if he'd like to forget his prisoner and start cleaning out the place.* HOPE *goes on pugnaciously.*

You stand up for your rights, bejees, Hickey! Don't let this smart-aleck dick get funny with you. If he pulls any rubber-hose tricks, you let me know! I've still got friends at the Hall! Bejees, I'll have him back in uniform pounding a beat where the only graft he'll get will be stealing tin cans from the goats!

MORAN

Furiously.

Listen, you cockeyed old bum, for a plugged nickel I'd—

Controlling himself, turns to HICKEY, *who is oblivious to all this, and yanks his arm.*

Come on, you!

HICKEY

With a strange mad earnestness.

Oh, I want to go, Officer. I can hardly wait now. I should have phoned you from the house right afterwards. It was a waste of time coming here. I've got to explain to Evelyn. But I know she's forgiven me. She knows I was insane. You've got me all wrong, Officer. I want to go to the Chair.

MORAN

Crap!

HICKEY

Exasperatedly.

God, you're a dumb dick! Do you suppose I give a damn about life now? Why, you bonehead, I haven't got a single damned lying hope or pipe dream left!

MORAN

Jerks him around to face the door to the hall.

Get a move on!

HICKEY

As they start walking toward rear—insistently.

All I want you to see is I was out of my mind afterwards, when I laughed at her! I was a raving rotten lunatic or I couldn't have said— Why, Evelyn was the only thing on God's earth I ever loved! I'd have killed myself before I'd ever have hurt her!

They disappear in the hall. HICKEY's *voice keeps on protesting.*

HOPE

Calls after him.

Don't worry, Hickey! They can't give you the Chair! We'll testify you was crazy! Won't we, fellers?

They all assent. Two or three echo HOPE's *"Don't worry, Hickey." Then from the hall comes the slam of the street door.* HOPE's *face falls—with genuine sorrow.*

He's gone. Poor crazy son of a bitch!

All the group around him are sad and sympathetic, too. HOPE *reaches for his drink.*

Bejees, I need a drink.

They grab their glasses. HOPE *says hopefully.*

Bejees, maybe it'll have the old kick, now he's gone.

He drinks and they follow suit.

ROCKY

Comes forward from where he has stood in the bar entrance—hopefully.
Yeah, Boss, maybe we can get drunk now.
He sits in the chair by CHUCK *and pours a drink and tosses it down.
Then they all sit still, waiting for the effect, as if this drink were a cru-
cial test, so absorbed in hopeful expectancy that they remain oblivious to
what happens at* LARRY'*s table.*

LARRY

His eyes full of pain and pity—in a whisper, aloud to himself.
May the Chair bring him peace at last, the poor tortured bastard!

PARRITT

Leans toward him—in a strange low insistent voice.
Yes, but he isn't the only one who needs peace, Larry. I can't feel
sorry for him. He's lucky. He's through, now. It's all decided for him.
I wish it was decided for me. I've never been any good at deciding
things. Even about selling out, it was the tart the detective agency
got after me who put it in my mind. You remember what Mother's
like, Larry. She makes all the decisions. She's always decided what I
must do. She doesn't like anyone to be free but herself.
He pauses, as if waiting for comment, but LARRY *ignores him.*
I suppose you think I ought to have made those dicks take me away
with Hickey. But how could I prove it, Larry? They'd think I was
nutty. Because she's still alive. You're the only one who can understand how guilty I am. Because you know her and what I've done to
her. You know I'm really much guiltier than he is. You know what
I did is a much worse murder. Because she is dead and yet she has
to live. For a while. But she can't live long in jail. She loves freedom
too much. And I can't kid myself like Hickey, that she's at peace. As
long as she lives, she'll never be able to forget what I've done to her
even in her sleep. She'll never have a second's peace.
He pauses—then bursts out.
Jesus, Larry, can't you say something?
LARRY *is at the breaking point.* PARRITT *goes on.*
And I'm not putting up any bluff, either, that I was crazy afterwards
when I laughed to myself and thought, "You know what you can

do with your freedom pipe dream now, don't you, you damned old bitch!"

LARRY

Snaps and turns on him, his face convulsed with detestation. His quivering voice has a condemning command in it.
Go! Get the hell out of life, God damn you, before I choke it out of you! Go up—!

PARRITT

His manner is at once transformed. He seems suddenly at peace with himself. He speaks simply and gratefully.
Thanks, Larry. I just wanted to be sure. I can see now it's the only possible way I can ever get free from her. I guess I've really known that all my life.
He pauses—then with a derisive smile.
It ought to comfort Mother a little, too. It'll give her the chance to play the great incorruptible Mother of the Revolution, whose only child is the Proletariat. She'll be able to say: "Justice is done! So may all traitors die!" She'll be able to say: "I am glad he's dead! Long live the Revolution!"
He adds with a final implacable jeer.
You know her, Larry! Always a ham!

LARRY

Pleads distractedly.
Go, for the love of Christ, you mad tortured bastard, for your own sake!
HUGO *is roused by this. He lifts his head and peers uncomprehendingly at* LARRY. *Neither* LARRY *nor* PARRITT *notices him.*

PARRITT

Stares at LARRY. *His face begins to crumble as if he were going to break down and sob. He turns his head away, but reaches out fumblingly and pats* LARRY's *arm and stammers.*
Jesus, Larry, thanks. That's kind. I knew you were the only one who could understand my side of it.
He gets to his feet and turns toward the door.

HUGO

Looks at PARRITT *and bursts into his silly giggle.*

Hello, leedle Don, leedle monkey-face! Don't be a fool! Buy me a trink!

PARRITT

Puts on an act of dramatic bravado—forcing a grin.

Sure, I will, Hugo! Tomorrow! Beneath the willow trees!

He walks to the door with a careless swagger and disappears in the hall. From now on, LARRY *waits, listening for the sound he knows is coming from the backyard outside the window, but trying not to listen, in an agony of horror and cracking nerve.*

HUGO

Stares after PARRITT *stupidly.*

Stupid fool! Hickey make you crazy, too.

He turns to the oblivious LARRY—*with a timid eagerness.*

I'm glad, Larry, they take that crazy Hickey avay to asylum. He makes me have bad dreams. He makes me tell lies about myself. He makes me want to spit on all I have ever dreamed. Yes, I am glad they take him to asylum. I don't feel I am dying now. He vas selling death to me, that crazy salesman. I think I have a trink now, Larry.

He pours a drink and gulps it down.

HOPE

Jubilantly.

Bejees, fellers, I'm feeling the old kick, or I'm a liar! It's putting life back in me! Bejees, if all I've lapped up begins to hit me, I'll be para-lyzed before I know it! It was Hickey kept it from— Bejees, I know that sounds crazy, but he was crazy, and he'd got all of us as bughouse as he was. Bejees, it does queer things to you, having to listen day and night to a lunatic's pipe dreams—pretending you believe them, to kid him along and doing any crazy thing he wants to humor him. It's dangerous, too. Look at me pretending to start for a walk just to keep him quiet. I knew damned well it wasn't the right day for it. The sun was broiling and the streets full of automobiles. Bejees, I could feel myself getting sunstroke, and an automobile damn near ran over me.

He appeals to ROCKY, *afraid of the results, but daring it.*

Ask Rocky. He was watching. Didn't it, Rocky?

ROCKY

A bit tipsily.

What's dat, Boss? Jees, all de booze I've mopped up is beginning to get to me.

Earnestly.

De automobile, Boss? Sure, I seen it! Just missed yuh! I thought yuh was a goner.

He pauses—then looks around at the others, and assumes the old kidding tone of the inmates, but hesitantly, as if still a little afraid.

On de woid of a honest bartender!

He tries a wink at the others. They all respond with smiles that are still a little forced and uneasy.

HOPE

Flashes him a suspicious glance. Then he understands—with his natural testy manner.

You're a bartender, all right. No one can say different.

ROCKY *looks grateful.*

But, bejees, don't pull that honest junk! You and Chuck ought to have cards in the Burglars' Union!

This time there is an eager laugh from the group. HOPE *is delighted.*

Bejees, it's good to hear someone laugh again! All the time that bas— poor old Hickey was here, I didn't have the heart— Bejees, I'm getting drunk and glad of it!

He cackles and reaches for the bottle.

Come on, fellers. It's on the house.

They pour drinks. They begin rapidly to get drunk now. HOPE *becomes sentimental.*

Poor old Hickey! We mustn't hold him responsible for anything he's done. We'll forget that and only remember him the way we've always known him before—the kindest, biggest-hearted guy ever wore shoe leather.

They all chorus hearty sentimental assent: "That's right, Harry!" "That's all!" "Finest fellow!" "Best scout!" etc. HOPE *goes on.*

Good luck to him in Matteawan! Come on, bottoms up!

They all drink. At the table by the window LARRY's *hands grip the edge of the table. Unconsciously his head is inclined toward the window as he listens.*

LARRY
Cannot hold back an anguished exclamation.
Christ! Why don't he—!

HUGO
Beginning to be drunk again—peers at him.
Vhy don't he what? Don't be a fool! Hickey's gone. He vas crazy. Have a trink.
Then as he receives no reply—with vague uneasiness.
What's matter vith you, Larry? You look funny. What you listen to out in backyard, Larry?
CORA *begins to talk in the group at right.*

CORA
Tipsily.
Well, I thank Gawd now me and Chuck did all we could to humor de poor nut. Jees, imagine us goin' off like we really meant to git married, when we ain't even picked out a farm yet!

CHUCK
Eagerly.
Sure ting, Baby. We kidded him we was serious.

JIMMY
Confidently—with a gentle, drunken unction.
I may as well say I detected his condition almost at once. All that talk of his about tomorrow, for example. He had the fixed idea of the insane. It only makes them worse to cross them.

WILLIE
Eagerly.
Same with me, Jimmy. Only I spent the day in the park. I wasn't such a damned fool as to—

LEWIS
Getting jauntily drunk.

Picture my predicament if I *had* gone to the Consulate. The pal of mine there is a humorous blighter. He would have got me a job out of pure spite. So I strolled about and finally came to roost in the park.

He grins with affectionate kidding at WETJOEN.

And lo and behold, who was on the neighboring bench but my old battlefield companion, the Boer that walks like a man—who, if the British Government had taken my advice, would have been removed from his fetid kraal on the veldt straight to the baboon's cage at the London Zoo, and little children would now be asking their nurses: "Tell me, Nana, is that the Boer General, the one with the blue behind?"

They all laugh uproariously. LEWIS *leans over and slaps* WETJOEN *affectionately on the knee.*

No offense meant, Piet, old chap.

WETJOEN

Beaming at him.

No offense taken, you tamned Limey!

WETJOEN *goes on—grinningly.*

About a job, I felt the same as you, Cecil.

At the table by the window HUGO *speaks to* LARRY *again.*

HUGO

With uneasy insistence.

What's matter, Larry? You look scared. What you listen for out there?

But LARRY *doesn't hear, and* JOE *begins talking in the group at right.*

JOE

With drunken self-assurance.

No, suh, I wasn't fool enough to git in no crap game. Not while Hickey's around. Crazy people puts a jinx on you.

MCGLOIN *is now heard. He is leaning across in front of* WETJOEN *to talk to* ED MOSHER *on* HOPE's *left.*

MCGLOIN

With drunken earnestness.

I know you saw how it was, Ed. There was no good trying to explain to a crazy guy, but it ain't the right time. You know how getting reinstated is.

MOSHER

Decidedly.

Sure, Mac. The same way with the circus. The boys tell me the rubes are wasting all their money buying food and times never was so hard. And I never was one to cheat for chicken feed.

HOPE

Looks around him in an ecstasy of bleery sentimental content.

Bejees, I'm cockeyed! Bejees, you're all cockeyed! Bejees, we're all all right! Let's have another!

They pour out drinks. At the table by the window LARRY *has unconsciously shut his eyes as he listens.* HUGO *is peering at him frightenedly now.*

HUGO

Reiterates stupidly.

What's matter, Larry? Why you keep eyes shut? You look dead. What you listen for in backyard?

Then, as LARRY *doesn't open his eyes or answer, he gets up hastily and moves away from the table, mumbling with frightened anger.*

Crazy fool! You vas crazy like Hickey! You give me bad dreams, too.

He shrinks quickly past the table where HICKEY *had sat to the rear of the group at right.*

ROCKY

Greets him with boisterous affection.

Hello, dere, Hugo! Welcome to de party!

HOPE

Yes, bejees, Hugo! Sit down! Have a drink! Have ten drinks, bejees!

HUGO

Forgetting LARRY *and bad dreams, gives his familiar giggle.*

Hello, leedle Harry! Hello, nice, leedle, funny monkey-faces!

Warming up, changes abruptly to his unusual declamatory denunciation.

Gottamned stupid bourgeois! Soon comes the Day of Judgment!

They make derisive noises and tell him to sit down. He changes again, giggling good-naturedly, and sits at rear of the middle table.

Give me ten trinks, Harry. Don't be a fool.

They laugh. ROCKY *shoves a glass and bottle at him. The sound of* MARGIE'S *and* PEARL'S *voices is heard from the hall, drunkenly shrill. All of the group turn toward the door as the two appear. They are drunk and look blowsy and disheveled. Their manner as they enter hardens into a brazen defensive truculence.*

MARGIE
Stridently.
Gangway for two good whores!

PEARL
Yeah! And we want a drink quick!

MARGIE
Glaring at ROCKY.
Shake de lead outa your pants, Pimp! A little soivice!

ROCKY
His black bullet eyes sentimental, his round Wop face grinning welcome.
Well, look who's here!
He goes to them unsteadily, opening his arms.
Hello, dere, Sweethearts! Jees, I was beginnin' to worry about yuh, honest!
He tries to embrace them. They push his arms away, regarding him with amazed suspicion.

PEARL
What kind of gag is dis?

HOPE
Calls to them effusively.
Come on and join the party, you broads! Bejees, I'm glad to see you!
The girls exchange a bewildered glance, taking in the party and the changed atmosphere.

MARGIE
Jees, what's come off here?

PEARL
Where's dat louse, Hickey?

ROCKY

De cops got him. He'd gone crazy and croaked his wife.

The girls exclaim, "Jees!" But there is more relief than horror in it.

ROCKY *goes on.*

He'll get Matteawan. He ain't responsible. What he's pulled don't mean nuttin'. So forget dat whore stuff. I'll knock de block off anyone calls you whores! I'll fill de bastard full of lead! Yuh're tarts, and what de hell of it? Yuh're as good as anyone! So forget it, see?

They let him get his arms around them now. He gives them a hug. All the truculence leaves their faces. They smile and exchange maternally amused glances.

MARGIE

With a wink.

Our little bartender, ain't he, Poil?

PEARL

Yeah, and a cute little Ginny at dat!

They laugh.

MARGIE

And is he stinko!

PEARL

Stinko is right. But he ain't got nuttin' on us. Jees, Rocky, did we have a big time at Coney!

HOPE

Bejees, sit down, you dumb broads! Welcome home! Have a drink! Have ten drinks, bejees!

They take the empty chairs on CHUCK's *left, warmly welcomed by all.* ROCKY *stands in back of them, a hand on each of their shoulders, grinning with proud proprietorship.* HOPE *beams over and under his crooked spectacles with the air of a host whose party is a huge success, and rambles on happily.*

Bejees, this is all right! We'll make this my birthday party, and forget the other. We'll get paralyzed! But who's missing? Where's the Old Wise Guy? Where's Larry?

ROCKY

Over by de window, Boss. Jees, he's got his eyes shut. De old bastard's asleep.

They turn to look. ROCKY *dismisses him.*

Aw, to hell wid him. Let's have a drink.

They turn away and forget him.

LARRY

Torturedly arguing to himself in a shaken whisper.

It's the only way out for him! For the peace of all concerned, as Hickey said!

Snapping.

God damn his yellow soul, if he doesn't soon, I'll go up and throw him off!—like a dog with its guts ripped out you'd put out of misery! *He half rises from his chair just as from outside the window comes the sound of something hurtling down, followed by a muffled, crunching thud.* LARRY *gasps and drops back on his chair, shuddering, hiding his face in his hands. The group at right hear it but are too preoccupied with drinks to pay much attention.*

HOPE

Wonderingly.

What the hell was that?

ROCKY

Aw, nuttin'. Someting fell off de fire escape. A mattress, I'll bet. Some of dese bums been sleepin' on de fire escapes.

HOPE

His interest diverted by this excuse to beef—testily.

They've got to cut it out! Bejees, this ain't a fresh-air cure. Mattresses cost money.

MOSHER

Now don't start crabbing at the party, Harry. Let's drink up.

HOPE *forgets it and grabs his glass, and they all drink.*

LARRY

In a whisper of horrified pity.

Poor devil!

A long-forgotten faith returns to him for a moment and he mumbles.
God rest his soul in peace.
He opens his eyes—with a bitter self-derision.
Ah, the damned pity—the wrong kind, as Hickey said! Be God, there's no hope! I'll never be a success in the grandstand—or anywhere else! Life is too much for me! I'll be a weak fool looking with pity at the two sides of everything till the day I die!
With an intense bitter sincerity.
May that day come soon!
He pauses startledly, surprised at himself—then with a sardonic grin.
Be God, I'm the only real convert to death Hickey made here. From the bottom of my coward's heart I mean that now!

HOPE
Calls effusively.
Hey there, Larry! Come over and get paralyzed! What the hell you doing, sitting there?
Then as LARRY *doesn't reply he immediately forgets him and turns to the party. They are all very drunk now, just a few drinks ahead of the passing-out stage, and hilariously happy about it.*
Bejees, let's sing! Let's celebrate! It's my birthday party! Bejees, I'm oreyeyed! I want to sing!
He starts the chorus of "She's the Sunshine of Paradise Alley," and instantly they all burst into song. But not the same song. Each starts the chorus of his or her choice. JIMMY TOMORROW's *is "A Wee Dock and Doris";* ED MOSHER's, *"Break the News to Mother";* WILLIE OBAN's, *the Sailor Lad ditty he sang in Act One;* GENERAL WETJOEN's, *"Waiting at the Church";* MCGLOIN's, *"Tammany";* CAPTAIN LEWIS's, *"The Old Kent Road";* JOE's, *"All I Got Was Sympathy";* PEARL's *and* MARGIE's, *"Everybody's Doing It";* ROCKY's, *"You Great Big Beautiful Doll";* CHUCK's, *"The Curse of an Aching Heart";* CORA's, *"The Oceana Roll"; while* HUGO *jumps to his feet and, pounding on the table with his fist, bellows in his guttural basso the French Revolutionary "Carmagnole." A weird cacophony results from this mixture and they stop singing to roar with laughter. All but* HUGO, *who keeps on with drunken fervor.*

HUGO

    Dansons la Carmagnole!

    Vive le son! Vive le son!

    Dansons la Carmagnole!

    Vive le son des canons!

They all turn on him and howl him down with amused derision. He stops singing to denounce them in his most fiery style.

Capitalist svine! Stupid bourgeois monkeys!

He declaims.

"The days grow hot, O Babylon!"

They all take it up and shout in enthusiastic jeering chorus.

"'Tis cool beneath thy willow trees!"

They pound their glasses on the table, roaring with laughter, and HUGO *giggles with them. In his chair by the window,* LARRY *stares in front of him, oblivious to their racket.*

CURTAIN

Eugene O'Neill (1888–1953) was born in New York City, the son of James O'Neill, a popular actor, and Mary Ellen Quinlan. During his childhood years he lived mainly in hotels with his family, following the tours of his father's company; the only permanent home the young O'Neill knew was a summer cottage in New London, Connecticut, which later became the setting for *Long Day's Journey into Night*.

As an adolescent, O'Neill attended eastern preparatory schools and then Princeton University for one year until he was expelled. During the next five years he worked as a gold prospector, a sailor, an actor, and a reporter.

O'Neill began writing plays in 1913, and by 1916 his one-act play *Bound East for Cardiff* was produced in New York by the Provincetown Players, a group he had helped found. In 1920 his full-length play *Beyond the Horizon* was produced in New York and won O'Neill the first of his four Pulitzer Prizes. During decades of extraordinary productivity, O'Neill published 24 other full-length plays. After receiving the Nobel Prize for literature in 1936, he published two of his most highly acclaimed plays, *The Iceman Cometh* and *A Moon for the Misbegotten*. O'Neill died in Boston in 1953. *Long Day's Journey into Night*, often regarded as his finest work, was published three years after his death.